FACE TO FACE

CREATING LIFELONG & MULTIGENERATIONAL CLIENTS

By Anthony J. DiLeonardi

Foreword by Scott Minerd
Global Chief Investment Officer, Guggenheim Partners

Copyright © 2014 Anthony J. DiLeonardi
All rights reserved.

ISBN: 1470021404
ISBN-13: 9781470021405
Library of Congress Control Number: 2014901583
CreateSpace Independent Publishing Platform
North Charleston, South Carolina

Publisher: Third Quarter Publications
Genre: Business and Money
For bulk sales of this product, please visit www.3qadvisers.com
Cover Design by Mary Leiser and Kimberly Medaglia

Printed in the United States of America

*Dedicated to my mom and dad, Dawn and Frank.
They taught me, through their humanness, how to love and forgive.*

ACKNOWLEDGMENTS

There is no way to adequately thank people in 500 words. It is my hope that everyone listed here, and those who are not, already know how thankful I am to have them in my life. If not, I have done a poor job of letting them know. However, let me specifically thank the following people who made this work possible. First and foremost I wish to thank Diane; you are a great wife and mother and truly my best friend. To Thea, James, Emma, and Ellie, you are my joy and every day I try to be better because of you. I am proud of you.

Dave and Jenifer Hooten, Mike and Donna Rigert, Greg and Amy Drake, I enjoy you in my life.

Stephanie DeMizio, Andy Andrews, Robert D. Smith, Chase Neely, Will Hoekenga, David Loy, Carl Hass, David Goetz and Scott Jeffery, you all are rock-solid coaches.

Kristan Wojnar, Sean DiLeonardi, and Thea DiLeonardi your professional editing, grammar, and content reviews were spot-on and helped this book come to life. If there is still an error, it's my fault.

Scott Minerd, thank you not just for the foreword but your solid, consistent example and wisdom. And to so many advisers who shared their stories, thank you for your vulnerability.

Mary Lieser and Kimberly Medaglia, thank you for your creativity on the cover design.

Finally, to the guys on the self-labeled "island of misfit toys:" Ray Chase, Lou Holland, Jay Hubbard, Stacey Huels, Tim Lefly, Matt Lorentsen, Chuck Meek, and Paul Negris—I thoroughly enjoy eating free lunches with you guys and being challenged and inspired by your intellect and passions.

TABLE OF CONTENTS

Foreword ix

Introduction xiii

Chapter One: Intimacy for the Wealth Adviser 1

Chapter Two: Creating a Culture of Intimacy 15

Chapter Three: Listen and Learn 27

Chapter Four: The Aging Population 41

Chapter Five: The Greatest Transfer of Wealth 51

Chapter Six: The Female Client 61

Chapter Seven: Your Competitive Advantage 75

Chapter Eight: Set Yourself Apart 85

Afterword 95

Advanced Praise for Face to Face 97

About the Author 101

FOREWORD

The job of a wealth adviser sounds straightforward—help build wealth for clients. You might think that job would be made easier after such strong performance as 2013 and that wealth advisers should be looking forward to updating their clients about performance. After all, in the business of building wealth, you would be excused for thinking that reviewing exceptional returns should be fun, especially when US stocks gained more than 30% in 2013.

But it is worth remembering that long-term wealth is not built by one week or one quarter of positive returns, nor is it destroyed by short periods of underperformance. In fact, 2013 is a good example of a period where investors took short a view on markets, and mutual fund inflows and outflows surged. By focusing on the long-term, advisers and their clients can avoid downside risks and damage.

Those flows from mutual fund investors over the past year reminded us just how tough the work of being a wealth adviser can be. Yes, US stocks had stellar gains, but investors were jittery. Some investors made rash changes to portfolios, while others took profits too early and missed a late-year surge in US equities. Some clients, despite strong performance, changed advisers because they had friends or colleagues whose advisers had achieved even stronger results in the near term. The jilted wealth adviser could be excused for being puzzled, left wondering why he lost a client, and wondering if any consideration was given to risk.

The past year serves as a reminder to wealth advisers that even during good times, investors can be fretful. So, what should you talk to clients about?

One answer is to talk about doing less, to remind clients to stay the course and not to chase the latest hot trend, since how frequently we react to market moves is a key factor in how our fortunes eventually fare. My friend and colleague Daniel Kahneman is a professor of psychology, and he won the Nobel Prize in economics in 2002 for his behavioral observations.

Among his best-known observations is that investors mark their portfolios to market too frequently. As he so aptly put it: "All of us would be better investors if we just made fewer decisions." Financial advisers must understand the long-term objectives of their clients and their ability to withstand short-term drawdowns—the best way to optimize the balance between risk and reward.

It is an approach that my friend and former colleague Tony DiLeonardi favors—never talk to clients about performance, do not try to win their attention with the latest fashionable trade, instead, work on building a better relationship by really getting to know the needs and desires of each client. The key to successful wealth management, Tony believes, is the right combination of portfolio management and a higher level of understanding the client.

I first met Tony in 2007 during the initial public offering for the Claymore/Guggenheim Strategic Opportunities Fund. We grew to know each other more closely in the period leading up to Guggenheim's subsequent acquisition of Claymore Securities and became friends. After the merger Tony worked on our efforts to train, develop, and educate wealth advisers on the noninvestment themes that were good for their business and their lives. It was an approach that followed the truism, "Give a man a fish, and he eats for a day. But teach him how to fish, and he will eat for life."

Tony's great strength has always been understanding relationships and how to foster the type of connection that keeps clients not just happy, but satisfied. Indeed, Tony's approach transcends the person to cultivate multigenerational clients by getting to know families, their culture, and what really makes them tick.

For Tony a lasting relationship is one that treats clients as human beings. Like many things in business, that is easier said than done because personal connections take real effort to develop and perhaps even more effort to maintain. Tony writes with modesty and from real-life experience about making those human connections and why relationships matter most. He explains how to create intimacy with clients, why happiness and personal growth is as important as money, and about what really matters—family, fun, and faith. This unique approach makes Tony stand out from the crowd as a coach to wealth advisers, and it is what makes this book worth reading.

In 2009, at the time of the Kentucky Derby, I summed up the macroeconomic outlook by telling clients that spring had arrived. Now as 2014 begins, the season is changing to summer and this is one of the best times in history to be an investor. Understanding the lessons Tony explains in the following pages will help you as a wealth adviser enjoy the summer, too.

Scott Minerd
Global Chief Investment Officer
Guggenheim Partners

January 2014

INTRODUCTION

Over the course of my career, those who know me well have called me Mr. Magoo. If you are under 40 years old, you may not be familiar with this cartoon character, who seemingly blind and usually lost, meandered through life with half-open eyes, feeling his way from one potentially dangerous situation to another. Ironically, those situations never backfired or cost him his life, but rather created opportunities.

Mr. Magoo's success came not because he had clear vision, all the correct answers, or even a keen sense of direction (although he did manage to continually move forward). It came rather because of his curious nature, walking through life with a purposeful mindset. He didn't always know where he was going, but along the way he discovered so many new, exciting, and productive opportunities and people that he literally stumbled across, that in turn led him to have more success and optimism.

For the first 10 years of my professional life, I was walking around like Mr. Magoo. I gravitated toward what I liked, trusting my gut, but never really had a direct plan for my future. Call it luck or divine intervention, but I somehow found myself on a path that would ultimately lead me to discover my true passion: **showing wealth advisers just like you how to create emotional intimacy, forge deeper connections, find purpose, and form lifelong and multigenerational relationships with the clients you serve.** I've been honored to spend the last 15 years speaking to and coaching over 10,000 wealth professionals across the country. It's been a privilege, and I'm grateful for having seized the opportunity to change the course of my life when I did.

GET CONSCIOUS, GAIN PRODUCTION

Hindsight being 20/20, I realize now that most of the improvements I have made in my personal and professional production came when I regained some form of consciousness, that is, when I paid close attention to others, noticed things and situations, asked questions, listened, and genuinely became interested again in people. Whenever I tap into my innate curiosity, I increase my state of awareness, which allows me to live with purpose and intention.

Are you walking around with your eyes barely open? Drifting through life unconsciously? Going from one item to the next on your daily to-do list? If you're reading this, you're most likely a professional who in some capacity builds, protects, or transfers wealth and legacy. I know it's not always easy, especially in our industry, to maintain a high level of awareness.

We live in a time where our focus is constantly being pulled in many directions. Between the demands of our family, business, and technology all vying for our attention, it can feel like there is no way to stay ahead. We are expected to keep up with the market, the latest trends, laws, funds, and innovations, not to mention world news, forecasts, and commentary, all so we can provide our clients with the best service, protect their assets, and continue to grow their portfolio. It's overwhelming to say the least.

I've been where you are. I have had the privilege of working with, for, and alongside so many interesting people for the last 25 years. My interactions with these people resulted in a desire for deeper, more meaningful relationships. I wanted to take off the blinders, go beyond the day-to-day, superficial conversations, and make purposeful choices for the future. Through this personal awakening, the idea of emotional intimacy was born.

In our ever-changing world, relationships matter most. People matter more than things. Relationships trump everything, even investment management, estate planning, accounting, and investment solutions. All of that is important, but not as important as the trusted relationship you either have or desire to have with the clients you serve.

Why do you need to create intimacy, how do you do it consistently, and what does it look like for the wealth and legacy professional today? These are legitimate and difficult questions.

INTRODUCTION

This book is my sincere attempt to highlight that topic based on years of calling on and serving wealth professionals and the clients they work hard with to build multigenerational wealth. Through my own shortcomings in this area and the experiences I've learned from so many professionals who believe what we do is a noble calling, I've come up with this simple, but I believe, profound approach to building intimacy in your wealth and legacy practice today that will do two things:

1. Change your life.
2. Change the lives of the clients you serve.

It is my desire that this book will help you in your noble calling. If you want to serve your clients with more honesty, integrity, and trust, this concept is for you. If you want to do that at the highest level you know how, this book will give you information, data, and ideas to serve your clients better and create stronger, generational relationships for years to come.

Why the title *Face to Face*? Like most of you, I have discovered, perhaps the hard way that the most productive, and perhaps life-changing, conversations I've had have come when I am face to face with someone. Whether it's with my wife on long drives or my children sitting on a pier or my colleagues as we get offsite for intentional time together, the results are profound. This idea hit me hard when I took my 18-year-old son on a five-day, 1,600-mile car trip to see four consecutive Major League Baseball (MLB) games together, in four different cities. This was a graduation gift to him, and I was excited as well because MLB is an interest we both share. Although we were looking out the front of the windshield for many of the miles, when we did talk, the conversations occurred organically over burgers at a food stop, when a certain song on the radio brought back a memory, or just when we'd both tell stories to go those last 20 miles. While covering that many miles in the car together was a stretch for us, it took us out of our usual environment and allowed us time to connect over a mutual passion. As my son gets older and moves on in life, I am grateful we took that trip because the memories will last forever.

I have often encouraged advisers that keeping a client happy may take what landed the client in the first place: a face-to-face meeting with her in her family room, not just in your office. Dynamics change when we go into a person's personal space and meet them face to face for genuine, purposeful dialogue. I can say with confidence that building multigenerational wealth and creating a legacy is a passion you share with 99.9% of your clients. So get out of the office and meet face to face in a place that will recharge your client's outlook for their future, encourage deeper conversation, and get you excited again for what you do.

Face to Face is about creating intimacy, and the outcome is to become an Intimate Wealth Adviser.

Mr. Magoo (From Wikipedia, the free encyclopedia)
Quincy Magoo (or simply Mr. Magoo) is a cartoon character created at the UPA animation studio in 1949, voiced by Jim Backus. In 2002, *TV Guide* ranked *Mr. Magoo* number 29 on its "50 Greatest Cartoon Characters of All Time" list. *TV Guide Book of Lists*. 158: Running Press. 2007. ISBN 0-7624-3007-9. (All rights reserved)

CHAPTER ONE
INTIMACY FOR THE WEALTH ADVISER

What thoughts come to mind when you hear the word intimacy? This may be a dangerous theme to open with because for many people, the word intimacy feels awkward or uncomfortable. For others, it's almost laughable. With the rise in popularity of personal development and self-help books, blogs, and TV shows, intimacy has become a mainstream buzzword. It's generally used in reference to male/female relationships. You know, you've seen the women's magazine article: "Six Ways to Improve Intimacy with Your Partner...Tonight." I think the word intimacy has gotten a bad rap simply because it's misunderstood, much like the term "affirmation" did back in the days of Stuart Smalley on *Saturday Night Live*. Remember his powerful affirmation? "I'm good enough, smart enough, and gosh darn it, people like me." We all had a good laugh and dismissed as nonsense what is actually a pretty useful development tool.

Same thing goes for intimacy. Many people have been turned off simply because of incorrect or over usage. So, before we go any further, I'm asking you to release any preconceived notions of intimacy. For us to build lifelong and multigenerational clients, we need it.

WHY INTIMACY?

I use intimacy for two reasons. First, it's because I truly believe it's the best word for what we are trying to create. And, secondly, because I feel it causes us to think. And isn't that really the definition of learning? After all, as professor and author Howard Hendricks said, "It's not what you think you are; rather it's what you think, you are."

If we look at the word intimate, it comes from the Latin *intima*, signifying the deepest, most internal part of something. The key word here to me is *something*. I argue that of all the service providers your clients have—as well as the prospective time-stealers and those attempting to add some value in the lives of your clients—your role and duty is the deepest, most internal part of their life. Not more important or deeper than their family or faith, perhaps, but certainly deeper and more internal than say, the mechanic, plumber, local politician, medical doctor, or nurse. Medical doctor? Really? Yes, perhaps even him or her.

> *What you do has the ability to go on for generation after generation*

There is one thing that each medical professional has in common. Eventually he or she will lose 100% of their clients, which he or she calls patients. Each one of them will die. But what you do, the trusted wealth professional, has the ability to go on for generation after generation. That's powerful.

In medicine, the intima is the inner lining of the arteries, the tunica interna, or inner coat. This joins with the endocardium, the inner lining of the heart. The intimate layer is the most profound and the most tender. To be intimate with another is to be open and uncover one's inner thoughts. We tend to do this with great anxiety and vulnerability, but that's exactly what is needed from you with your best clients to create the mutual intimacy that leads to lifelong relationships and passes to future generations.

WHY DOES INTIMACY MATTER?

The data and the told and untold stories of this industry indicate that most of your clients don't feel that you care about them, their family and their needs. You may care about the size of their wealth, the products they use, and the "suitability" for those products. Consider this:

- 98% of adult children switch financial advisers once they have received their inheritance from their parents. ("Engaging and Retaining Families," *Investments & Wealth Monitor*, IMCA, September/October 2011)
- On average, affluent clients with more than $5M in assets have seven advisers in their lifetime.
- 25% of the affluent claim they are looking for a new "planner" not because of performance, but rather, lack of contact. (Phoenix Wealth Management Survey, Harris Poll, 2002)

Therefore, intimacy in your practice with your best clients matters because it's how you will perform your noble calling, attract and keep your clients, and inherit more clients because of not just what you do for them, but how you do it.

In journalist Malcolm Gladwell's book *Blink* (Back Bay Books, 2005), he looks at medical professionals and their likelihood of being sued for malpractice. The net of the example is those medical professionals whose patients consider them to have a favorable bedside manner, regardless of their technical proficiency and competency of the MD, were less likely to be sued for malpractice than those doctors who had real or perceived bad bedside manner. He found out that in many cases, the patient's feelings of a good bedside manner versus a bad bedside manner came from just three minutes more of dialogue (connection) with the patient. That was from 15 minutes to 18 minutes of intimacy. A bit of interest, compassion, and concern from the doctor created a much healthier, productive, and profitable relationship. It was not just the medicine; it was also the relationship.

So, three more minutes of genuine, caring conversation means a doctor is less likely to be sued than a doctor who is technically more proficient, but perceived as less caring, compassionate, and does not take the time to know his or her patient. What does this have to do with you, the wealth professional? Everything. I believe this example is absolutely transferable to your business and our industry. We need to improve our bedside manner (our intimacy) for all the right reasons.

YOUR NOBLE CALLING

A wealth adviser is the professional who creates, protects, and transfers wealth and legacy for the clients they serve. The key word here is adviser. Through your confidence and direction, you help your clients plan and build generational wealth and legacy for today and tomorrow. It has the ability to outlive your current client's lifespan and move on to future generations. That includes, but certainly is not limited to, retirement funding, higher education, and comfortable living both now and at the end of one's life on earth. It includes funding and protecting trusts, estates, vacation homes, and philanthropic desires. It means building and codifying legacy and contributing to those who need help. It means teaching stewardship.

> **We need to create intimacy now**

The wealth advisers today are the women and men who help clients create, protect, and transfer wealth through the financial intermediaries, insurance providers, planners, estate and trust lawyers, bankers, and certified public accountants, to name a few. I firmly believe that funding people's retirements, helping them buy second homes, funding their children's higher education, and building generational wealth is noble. Would you agree?

What you do matters. You assist clients in building, planning, and funding dreams. You also help those dreams cross over to the next generation. As I said, not even a medical professional can do that. Amazing, isn't it?

WHAT IS WEALTH?

What does wealth mean to you? Quick, top-of-the-mind answer.

Some people think wealth is about money or being rich in material possessions. For my purpose I desire to keep it simple. You are rich with an abundance of friends, love, family, experiences, and joy. How about being wealthy because you have an education, great health and plenty of free time? That's wealth to me. Wealth to me is human intimacy and connection.

When I ask men and women what wealth is to them, I always get different answers. Men typically answer with a goal in mind (i.e., lake house, college funding) and women will tend to answer with words like freedom and security. These are very different answers to the same question. So what does this tell us? Well, for starters it makes it clear that women look at wealth in terms of life values, not just the value of the wealth, highlighting the significance of the emerging values-based conversation.

Like success, there can be many definitions for wealth. I personally love the word abundance. It's become quite a catchword lately. Since the debut of the movie *The Secret* in 2006, the idea of scarcity versus abundance has exploded. Of course, these concepts have been around for ages, but they continue to receive wide interest and appeal even today. In basic terms, scarcity is living in the mindset of lack, the fear of never having enough or losing it all. On the flip side, there is abundance, living the life you love, always having and creating more.

Do you live your life in abundance or scarcity? Do you believe that there are enough resources for everyone or do you feel there is a limited supply? How do your beliefs influence your practice? How does your mindset affect your clients?

In her book, *The Soul of Money* (W.W. Norton & Co., 2006), global activist, fundraiser, and speaker Lynne Twist introduces an alternative to this scarcity and abundance consciousness and demonstrates how we can replace feelings of scarcity, guilt, and burden with experiences of sufficiency, freedom, and purpose. She writes, "Once we let go of scarcity, we discover the surprising truth of sufficiency. By sufficiency, I don't mean a quantity of anything. Sufficiency isn't two steps up from poverty or one step short of abundance. Sufficiency is...a knowing that there is enough, and that we are enough." She goes on, "When we live in the context of sufficiency, we find a natural freedom and integrity. We engage in life from a sense of our own wholeness rather than a desperate longing to be complete. We feel naturally called to share the resources that flow through our lives—our time, our money, our wisdom, our energy, at whatever level those resources flow—to serve our highest commitments." Wow. What would happen if you engaged this approach with yourself, your family, and your clients? I'll give you a hint: intimacy.

I've become convinced that so many wealth professionals that I have met have the desire to create intimacy, but because they are knee-deep in running a dynamic practice, they don't know what to do. Let's see, you manage hundreds of clients, you build portfolios, stay in tune to the markets and the laws. You provide advice on tax questions and estate questions. You meet with and stay on top of too many product providers. You answer servicing questions about updated zip codes and going paperless. You prospect and you run a team. Oh, and you have a personal life, too.

Think about where you are in your life and your practice. How would your employees or clients describe you? What is your identity? Do they know you intimately? What do you do to foster more meaningful interactions with them?

Even better, who are your clients? What are their dreams? Are you tuned in to their needs, wants, and concerns?

WHAT'S AT STAKE?

In his book, *Fired Up or Burned Out* (Thomas Nelson Inc., 2007), consultant and speaker Michael Lee Stallard shows us that employee disengagement is a widespread malady in American organizations, causing the loss of billions of dollars, hours of dissatisfaction, and work lives lacking true value. Research shows that in the average organization, 75% of employees are just showing up for the paycheck. They are not giving their best efforts or aligning their behavior with organizational goals. These are your clients and prospects. They may even be, unfortunately, you and your own team members.

People are frustrated, disheartened, and just going through the motions. They need you, the intimate wealth adviser, to show them a compelling future.

The evidence points to a national concern and an alarming statistic. Some of the most compelling work has come from the Corporate Leadership Council, "Driving Performance and Retention Through Employee Engagement" (Washington DC, Corporate Executive Board, 2004). In America today, there is a decline in joy. That is, more adult Americans say they are less happy today than they were five years ago, 10 years ago. This staggering and disturbing trend has been in effect since just after World War II. Furthermore, this trend has occurred during the greatest economic prosperity in the country's history. It reminds us that it's not just about money. There is more going on here. Another profound body of work on this decline in corporate and personal joy comes from The Gallup Organization Q12 Survey. Google it; it's worth the read.

I believe this stated decline in joy could be attributed to many things. At the core, in my opinion, is diminished intimacy. Certainly, the following demographic and cultural changes are key contributors to this phenomenon:

- Geographical spread
- Two-career couples
- Increased hours in the workplace
- Technology
- Stress
- Economic pressures

When people—you, me, your clients—enter a new organization or relationship, we tend to be excited, engaged, and fired up about that new experience and what it may lead to. There is a newness that outweighs the anxiety to the experience or relationship. It also causes us to be on guard, to be conscious of what we say, plan, and do. Typically, those are good things. If you doubt that, I'd ask you to consider your personal relationships. How did you feel when those relationships started? If you are married, did you enter this relationship engaged, energized, and intrigued? Of course you did. And that led to a better relationship where genuine listening and compassion took place.

Over time, however, the environment around us reduces that flame of excitement and engagement into a flicker, often times barely noticeable and at the risk of being extinguished. When I say environment I mean things like business cycles, the markets, new laws, compliance, deadlines, tax changes, bad communication, stress, and power plays, to name just a few. How about in your family: aging, retirement, illness, raising children, college tuitions, and staying happily married. That engagement you had earlier is not always there after 20 years of marriage. This leads to difficult situations and feelings of brokenness. There are environmental issues all around us vying for our time and emotions. These issues, if left unchecked, will create havoc in our relationships and well-being. I know this to be true because it happened to me.

In early 2008, at what could be considered the height of my career, I was frustrated, burnt out, and desperate. I was in a senior executive leadership position at a fast-growing, privately held company with 120 sales people, roughly 50% of all employees, indirectly reporting to me and controlling more than 50% of the firm's revenues. Under today's standards for success, I should have been happy and fulfilled, but instead I grew increasingly restless. I stopped taking calls. When I did communicate, I found myself using destructive language toward my team, people I interviewed and hired, that I never should have used. I didn't like what was happening, and I had to take a step back. I was at a crucial crossroad and luckily, my Mr. Magoo days were far behind me, and I took the next step with my eyes wide open.

I've never been particularly enthralled with financial services. I was never in love with the market, and I'm still not. I do have enormous respect for the complexity of the industry and the professionals who dominate it, but the numbers game doesn't excite me. So why am I still so deeply invested in wealth management? I am, and will always be, a student of the sales process and human nature. I am interested in the story, the relationship, and the dream. The financial services industry, wealth management, investment, and securities, insurance, accounting, and legal services—whatever you want to call it—at its core, is about heart, soul, and prosperity. It is indeed noble work, and I'm privileged to be a part of it.

It was because of this belief that the work we do is noble, that I marched into my colleague's office, looked him in the eye, and shared my vision. We needed a group within our organization that would help financial professionals build a better practice and have a better life. With an energy and passion I hadn't felt in a long time, I took the helm and charted my course.

A SENSE OF COMMUNITY

Looking back, I am fortunate that my company embraced my initiative and supported my efforts. It could have gone in the complete opposite direction and ended terribly. I've seen it firsthand; lost relationships, depleted energy, and too much time in conflict resolution wreak a well-documented emotional toll and an obvious financial charge to this cycle. In our business today, these types of situations will lead to:

- Lost production
- High turnover
- Reduced revenue
- Dysfunctional teams

In the book, *This Land of Strangers* (Greenleaf Book Group Press, 2012), author Robert E. Hall suggests our relationships are collapsing. It is the crisis that everyone feels, but that has gone unnamed. We see the pieces: broken families, communities in chaos, education in disarray, business losing the trust of customers and employees, and political discourse that sows dysfunction and divide.

He documents that these broken relationships have a death grip on economic, political, and social advancements that capitalism, democracy, social programs, and tax policy have been unable to break. Cumulatively, this crisis feeds an emerging caste system: individuals and organizations that possess superior relationships *have*, while those with deteriorating relationships are destined to *have not*.

FACE TO FACE

We've seen it before, when it looks like we are at an enormous cultural divide and our relationships are shattered with no hope of compromise, something happens that shakes us up and brings us together. I'm confident you recall exactly where you were that Tuesday morning, September 11, 2001. Our country was caught in the most unimaginable turmoil and yet, immediately, community became so critical. Even if you did not live or work in the New York City area or near Washington DC, you desired, sought, and built community. In the days following that senseless and devastating attack, we came together in our neighborhoods, in business, and in families.

In September 2001, I was transitioning from a job that had my family and I based in Toronto, Canada. I had moved my wife and young children back to the Chicago area in late August and continued my role in Toronto (for the US-based company I was working with at the time). I was commuting for the final four months from Chicago to Toronto, flying up each Monday and returning each Friday evening. I flew up Monday, September 10, 2001. I, like many of you, watched in horror on the television the next morning as the news unfolded that tragic day. Once I knew that my friends and colleagues in New York and Washington DC were safe, I sat back that evening and realized I needed to be home. I needed to be home with my family and friends. Just home. Of course I could not get home for days. I could not fly and the borders were closed. I've never had a feeling of isolation like that before. I have never sensed a lack of community like that and don't desire to ever again. I do want to say, Canadians were awesome. They were sympathetic and hospitable. But nearly all my personal community was back in Chicago, and that's where I needed to be.

I recall being in New York City months later and New Yorkers still desired to talk about those days as a form of healing and to fulfill community. This concept became painfully clear to me at the time: we must connect with others to thrive. Stallard and others have eloquently, and with great alarm, put it out there as well for all to see.

That's what's at stake, and that's why I use the word intimacy to define what you, the intimate wealth adviser, does and equally important, what your best clients desire.

THE OPPORTUNITY

Do you believe that if you could create openness and a deeper sense of trust with your clients, you would have a tremendously better relationship with them? Do you believe what you do matters? Do you find purpose in what you do for your clients that causes you to want to do more? That's intimacy. That's a noble calling. If we, as an industry of wealth professionals serving clients each day, can capture that, our business and industry will surely benefit greatly.

In internationally esteemed psychologist Martin Seligman's book, *Flourish* (Simon and Schuster, 2011), we learn of his dynamic new concept of what well-being really is. Traditionally, the goal of psychology has been to relieve human suffering, but the goal of the Positive Psychology movement, which Dr. Seligman has led for 15 years, is different—it's about actually raising the bar for the human condition.

> **Do you believe what you do matters?**

Flourish builds on Seligman's game-changing work on optimism, motivation, and character to show how to get the most out of life, unveiling an electrifying new theory of what makes a good life for individuals, communities and nations. In a fascinating evolution of thought and practice, *Flourish* refines what Positive Psychology is all about.

While certainly a part of well-being, happiness alone doesn't give life meaning. Seligman now asks what is it that enables you to cultivate your talents, to build deep, lasting relationships with others, to feel pleasure, and to contribute meaningfully to the world? In a word, what is it that allows you to flourish? Well-being takes the stage front and center and Happiness (or Positive Emotion) becomes one of the five pillars of Positive Psychology, along with Engagement, Relationships, Meaning, and Accomplishment or PERMA, the permanent building blocks for a life of profound fulfillment.

So many people look at happiness as the final destination on this journey. "I'll be happy when/if." But the key is to find happiness during the ups and downs, the uncertainty, and the unknown. If happiness is all we strive for, we really are missing out on a range of other emotions and experiences. What about courage? In the face of adversity, there is something to be said for bravery, faith, and resolve. How about compassion? Being thoughtful, having empathy, and sharing strength are an integral part of the human experience. Loyalty, hope, optimism, and most of all, love, are what get us through any and every situation. This idea is based on science and years of study by leading professionals in the worlds of business, psychology, sociology, and physiology.

The folks at Harvard University Medical School have shown us research that says babies who are held, stroked, and cuddled are healthier than babies who aren't given that tender touch. Adolescents connected at home and at school are well adjusted and have a greater likelihood of passing grades. Patients with greater social support recover faster than those who go it alone. Adults with more social relationships are less prone to sickness, depression, and suicide. And finally, seniors with more relationships live longer. Don't you desire for yourself and your clients a longer, healthier life? There's also a business reason why you want an older, healthier client, correct? Let's not hide the fact that there is a practical business reason behind this as well. It's OK. When you add value, when you make someone's life better, you should get paid. There, I said it and now we can move on.

John F. Kennedy said, "Change is the law of life. And those who look only to the past or present are certain to miss the future." Sometimes we must force change upon ourselves to see new opportunities. If we think it's difficult, it is. But doing the same thing in an ever-changing world is insanity, and it's uninspiring as well.

Action Exercise: Sit somewhere comfortable and answer the following questions from a place of honesty and conviction. Be vulnerable and really put yourself out there. These answers are for you alone and will help you lead with intention and serve your clients at a higher level.

1. What do I do?

_____

_____

_____

_____

_____

2. What is my purpose?

_____

_____

_____

_____

_____

3. What do my clients want?

_____

_____

_____

_____

4. How can I serve my clients? How can I better their lives?

_____
_____
_____
_____
_____
_____

Creating lifelong, multigenerational clients is a focus on two-way relationships and a better communication strategy. It is not "segmenting your book." It is relationship management to the next level. It is not product solution pitches, fee schedule changes, or investment management discussions. It's about being intentional and practical in your day-to-day client relationships. It's about connecting with those clients and prospects that you want to have a deeper relationship with. It's about building a brand that is based on a culture that finds, attracts, and keeps employees and customers connected and wanting more. It's about intimacy.

CHAPTER TWO
CREATING A CULTURE OF INTIMACY

How can we create, or in many cases recreate, an intentional culture of intimacy to enhance productivity? The simplest way to do that is to do something different. Doing things different than before often leads to new perspectives, which usually lead to new opportunities. New opportunities inspire thinking, action, and lead to new production levels.

Early in my career, I was attending the top producer's conference for a large regional broker. I was one of 40 fund company representatives presenting to 250 or so top financial advisers—who at that time, were the best of the best. For three days we all sat together and listened as 40 asset managers presented their story and sold their products from the main stage. I can honestly say that out of 40 presentations, 35 were terrible. The two main factors that made me come to that conclusion were:

1. Presentation Skills: They lacked the ability to capture and engage the audience.
2. Content: The vast majority of presenters focused solely on the performance of their product.

I left that conference with two declarations:

1. I can present better.
2. I wouldn't sell based on the performance of a fund.

The first declaration was easy enough to fulfill with study and practice. The second took some serious thought. You see, the old model of presenting was based on a promise, and to be frank, was out of my control. How could I ensure a top-performing fund today, last month, or last year would continue that same way? By selling on performance, I'm giving my advisers the right to fire me if everything doesn't play out as I say. Talk about pressure.

I knew I had to figure out a different method to sell in the industry that went beyond the traditional sales model. Having only been on the job for six weeks at that point, I came up with a plan and made my third declaration:

3. I'm going to help financial advisers be better practitioners, grow their business, and manage their life.

No small feat, but I was ready. I took on a completely different mindset in my approach to doing business. My focus became less about the product and more about the producer and the culture of the industry itself.

What's exciting about this strategy is that many successful companies are doing it today with extraordinary results. Take a look at Google: They have created not only a unique culture, but also a movement. At the core of their business model is that happy employees are productive employees. Google takes care of its people. They have built a campus where any need you could ever have—in work and in life—is addressed. From meals, to healthcare, to dry cleaning—all your bases are covered at Google. Source: http://blog.kissmetrics.com/googles-culture-of-success/.

Another company that has created an amazing culture for its employees and its clients is Zappos Their business practices are so transparent, they

CREATING A CULTURE OF INTIMACY

have their 10 core family values listed right there on their website. Source: http://about.zappos.com/our-unique-culture/zappos-core-values.

1. Deliver WOW Through Service
2. Embrace and Drive Change
3. Create Fun and a Little Weirdness
4. Be Adventurous, Creative, and Open Minded
5. Pursue Growth and Learning
6. Build Open and Honest Relationships with Communication
7. Build a Positive Team and Family Spirit
8. Do More with Less
9. Be Passionate and Determined
10. Be Humble

What are your core values for your business? I encourage you to think this through and come up with what really drives you to do what you do for yourself, your employees, and your clients.

A PURPOSEFUL PRACTICE

When I was at that crossroad back in 2008, I was asking the same tough questions that I've proposed to you: what's my purpose? What is the purpose of all of this? What does success look like? During one of my conversations with a colleague, he asked me, "What would make you loosen the grip on the steering wheel every morning?" That's an insightful question, because when we're stressed and headed toward burnout, we grip that wheel so hard. We can't see beyond that day's challenges. Our focus is on survival. I believe that breathing room—and opportunity—comes from doing something radically different. That's what I told him and that's what I eventually did. And you know what happened? When I gave myself permission to explore another idea or perspective, I loosened that grip on the steering wheel. I began to think in ways I had never expected.

I have never regretted the decision I made to leave my post. I've never looked back. I took some time to examine what I knew I could not and would not do anymore. Then, I looked at what I thought was needed and you know what I discovered? It was time to put my skin in the game. Take a risk. Bet on myself. Sure, I had people tell me they were worried about me. By giving up managing 50% of the employees who generated 50% of the company's revenue, overnight I became a cost, not a revenue creator. While some saw me as a liability, I never felt more liberated.

I still remember the day that I created the foundation for a program that I would ultimately present, manage, and direct for five years. It was a program that exceeded expectations and withstood—and prevailed—during an unstable economy and later, through a company acquisition. But that first morning, when I sat in my home at the kitchen table, letting the weight of what I had done sink in, I felt a spark. I became energized. I started to write and got in total flow. When I finally looked up, it was the afternoon and I was still at the computer pounding away.

YOUR COMPETITIVE ADVANTAGE

Do you want to feel that burst of adrenaline, that sense of purpose, drive, and passion? Then do something different and be open to the possibilities. It doesn't mean you have to leave your current position. You don't need to do anything drastic that will jeopardize what you've worked for and built in your life. Sometimes it's the subtle changes implemented over time that make a huge impact. I've taken both approaches at different times in my career and created major transformations with each. But whether you go slow and steady or swift and spontaneous, you do need to leave doubt behind and embrace the idea of change—in your beliefs, in your approach, and in your service to your clients.

It's a competitive advantage for the wealth manager who embraces doing things differently

To me, this is not just a better way to live, which it is. It's a competitive advantage for the wealth manager who embraces it and does things differently with the clients you serve and the team you manage. I also believe the time for us in this service industry is now. Intimacy is real, personal, and long lasting. Do we want to create a vibrant personal connection with the clients we serve for generations? Why then do we allow other industry professionals less important to the day-to-day significance of

CREATING A CULTURE OF INTIMACY

our clients seemingly command more personal intimacy and loyalty than we do?

As a test, I encourage you to name some examples of retail businesses that you are a customer of that you believe understand intimacy and deliver on experience for you. Think of a company or organization that you feel strongly about and for whom you have a sense of loyalty. What comes to mind? How long did it take before you were out of names? My guess is you came up with about six or seven.

In my asking that question to thousands of wealth advisers, I find it amusing that just six names or so come up very regularly and not one of them is a big bank, brokerage house, insurance agency, law firm, or accounting firm.

Here's what usually comes up:

- Starbucks
- Nordstrom
- The Ritz Carlton
- Southwest Airlines
- Apple
- Amazon
- Zappos

Over the last several years, I've compared the results of *Business Week's* annual Customer Service Champs and found they were basically the same names I would hear from audiences of seasoned professional wealth managers. The other interesting thing is there does not seem to be a lot of businesses that really get this service loyalty model anymore. The list is narrow and not so deep.

With the exception of Charles Schwab, I've not seen many wealth companies on the list. You might say that's because they are too big. OK. But what makes our industry appealing and your practice effective, in part, is the fact that you have the ability to be independent, build your own brand, and construct a client base that buys from YOU. You are your brand. That's liberating and powerful.

Let's consider Starbucks for a minute. They get this concept of intimacy. They're big, but their raving fans feel like the barista cares deeply about them. Howard Schultz, CEO at Starbucks, has said publically the following, Starbucks sells connection; connection to self, to colleague, and to community. Did you catch that? Starbucks sells connection, which to me is intimacy. I thought they sold coffee and scones. They seem to move a lot of coffee and scones in their stores. Yet the CEO said they sell intimacy, and oh by the way, if you want to plop down $5 for a coffee, you can do that, too. Wow.

In the book, *Starbucks Experience* (McGraw Hill Companies, 2007), by business consultant Joseph Michelli, we learn the valuable lessons and the genius of Starbucks's success lies in its ability to create personalized customer experiences, stimulate business growth, generate profits, energize employees and secure customer loyalty-all at the same time.

Here's my plea. Why should our retail business be any different? Why should we allow Starbucks, for example, to create intimacy, loyalty, and a raving fan base when they do not really provide anything that's noble, lasting, or significant? Yet they do provide value in the life of their customers by offering intimacy and a warm place to sit, sip, and become part of a community. Why can't we get this? As a matter of fact, they can charge a premium for their product because they provide intimacy and the rest. Think about it.

This example, and others like it, proves to me that this is more than customer service. This is an intentional strategy from Schultz; he himself said it. It's a culture. There are countless stories of their baristas building meaningful relationships with customers. It also tells me that it's more than corporate branding or millions of dollars in national advertising, because this is done at the grassroots level, in community after community. Sound familiar to you? That should be encouraging since your practice is a grassroots practice that does not need national advertising budgets and an expensive branding campaign.

Finally, it tells me that this concept of creating intimacy and personal connection with your clients is manageable and portable. It takes efforts and intentionality and it can be done in store after store across the country. You just have to do it in your one location.

PROFESSIONAL PRODUCTIVITY, PERSONAL HAPPINESS

What this concept of creating intimacy is all about is a combination of both professional productivity and personal happiness. Building lifelong, multigenerational clients through more meaningful and purposeful connection is all about you, as well as the clients you serve. It will do the following:

- Boost morale
- Increase productivity
- Retain assets, contracts, and satisfied customers
- Support growth
- Decrease turned-over relationships, both in your business and on your team

This concept of human connection is meaningful. Simply Google the word *bond* and see what pops up. (Besides James Bond, code name 007. Just making sure you are paying attention.)

Is it your business objective to secure influence or importance with your best clients? I hope so. Are you better equipped to add value, build a meaningful wealth portfolio, or plan an estate if you have influence over your clients? Absolutely. Do you desire them to view you as important in their life? Of course you do.

American psychologist Dr. Abraham Maslow made it simple. To paraphrase, when humans are in a well-connected intimate relationship, we have our basic human psychological needs met:

- Respect
- Recognition
- Belonging
- Autonomy

- Personal Growth
- Meaning or Purpose

When these basic human needs are met, Maslow continued, we now accept that we as humans thrive and are:

- More productive
- More innovative
- More profitable
- Better problem solvers
- More trusting and trusted

Wow, that is huge! By simply meeting the basic human psychological needs described above—or said differently, by having intimacy with others—we, as humans, are more productive, innovative, profitable, creative, and trusting. Is that a list of attributes that you desire for yourself, for your clients, and for your friends and colleagues? And really, when it comes right down to your business, are you in the business of TRUST? Don't you want your clients and team members to trust you more while you trust them? This is it.

TOUGH QUESTIONS

I've long said that the key to a productive and successful sales and service model is three-pronged. The professional that hits high levels of production and stays at high levels of production must:

1. Be a student of the market they serve.
2. Be a student of the sales process, that is, the human and political stages in which clients and prospects find themselves throughout the relationship.
3. Create "likeability" with clients and prospects, and ultimately, that likeability must lead *to "trustability."*

Because of that three-pronged approach, I have created deeper, more purposeful relationships in my own practice and taught others how to do the same in theirs.

Look, I know you're busy. I've been where you are. Not only have I heard the excuses, I've used them myself. Life is a juggling act, but it's time to rid your self of the feeling that disaster will strike if one ball falls. Find your footing. Be purposeful in your choices. Be honest. When you think about your average day, how much time do you spend on your business? You read the paper to stay up on trends, watch the news for the latest numbers, but how much time do you devote to your professional goals? What plans do you make for cultivating and strengthening relationships? You must have a daily practice. Make this reflection part of your morning ritual. Every day, focus on how you can better meet the needs of your clients, encourage workplace production, and foster an environment that promotes happiness. In other words, think about opportunities to go face to face. You can succeed in sales if you are liked. You will succeed in lifelong, multigenerational sales if you are trusted.

Action Exercise: It's time to ask some even tougher questions. Spend at least 10 minutes of quiet time answering these questions, thinking of clients that come to mind, and planning on doing something to either change the course or make the relationship even better.

1. What client have I lost intimacy with recently?

_____
_____
_____

2. Why did I lose that intimacy?

_____
_____
_____

3. What could I have done differently?

_____
_____
_____

4. Which clients have lost intimacy with me?

_____
_____
_____

5. What will I do to initiate contact and improve intimacy with these clients?

_____
_____
_____

Remember, intimacy is not a one-way street. There are two parties involved in every relationship, and it may be worth asking your clients these questions. They most likely will tell you. Just be ready to really listen to their answers.

CHAPTER THREE

LISTEN AND LEARN

Listen and learn. I was reminded of this simple, yet powerful concept when I had the privilege to meet face to face with Ernie Banks. If you don't know him, Ernie played professional baseball for 19 years for one team, one owner, in one city, for one mayor, in one stadium, under one light—the sun. He is "Mr. Cub." He is a member of the Baseball Hall of Fame, The 500 Home Run Club, and his number is retired from the Chicago Cubs and hangs on the foul pole in Wrigley Field. He is known for his optimism and positive spirit, and I am honored to know him.

I have learned many great lessons from Ernie. One in particular really stuck with me, even more so after I viewed the blockbuster movie *42*.

42, as you may know, is the retired number of baseball great, Jackie Robinson. Jackie was the first African American to break the all-white baseball barrier in 1947. The Major Leagues had not had an African American player since 1889, when baseball became segregated. When Jackie first donned a Brooklyn Dodger uniform, he pioneered the integration of professional athletics in America. By breaking the color barrier in baseball, the nation's preeminent sport, he courageously challenged the deeply rooted custom of racial segregation in both the North and the South. As a result of his great success, Jackie was eventually inducted into the Baseball Hall of Fame in 1962.

So what did Mr. Banks tell me that I believe is helpful to intimate wealth advisers today? He shared with me what Jackie Robinson told him one day in 1953 when Jackie, while on a day off, visited Ernie face to face at Wrigley Field in his rookie year. Jackie sought Ernie out and simply said, "Just listen and learn, Ernie." I asked Ernie what he said back to Jackie. Ernie's response? "Nothing, I just listened and learned." Poetic.

These words are so powerful. Perhaps if we desire more wisdom, better client relationships, and greater production and results, we should just listen and learn more. Listen to our clients. Listen to our team members and get intentionally engaged in meaningful client relationships with purpose again.

DEFINING WEALTH MANAGEMENT

Research is clear, when the affluent client is asked what they want most from their adviser, they reply with a more robust service model and the fact that they want to be heard. Consider this:

- When the affluent are asked what they want from the financial services sector: 77% say wealth management.
- When they were asked what they perceived they got from the sector: 81% say product push. (Source: Phoenix Wealth Management Survey, Harris Poll, 2002)

What does wealth management mean? To me, and I think to countless numbers of your clients, it means concierge service. It means help me have a better, more comfortable life. It does not mean jam more product and market insight at me. Stop selling products and begin selling you as the trusted adviser—the one person who can make my life better.

Let me explain it this way. I believe there are three types of people walking around God's great planet. I will, for this example, label them as follows:

- Intentional Disconnector
- Unintentional Connector
- Intentional Connector

In this nonscientific, but radically practical example, the Intentional Disconnector is the person who deliberately wreaks havoc on relationships. He/she is constantly complaining, creating conflict, and looking for fights. They seek to destroy relationships. They are often times the "victim." The good news is that this group of people represents the vast minority; let's say 10%. If they are your employees or clients, fire them. If they are in your family, God bless you.

The Unintentional Connector represents that largest group of people; let's say 80% of the population. These are good intentioned, hardworking men and women who simply by being alive, conscious, and active in their life are connecting people to people and creating mainly positive relationships. The challenge here is that this group is doing it unintentionally. The results are good, but they are unaware of the power of what they are doing in life.

Therefore, the "power" position is the Intentional Connector, defined as practical and aware that relationships matter, they drive results and understand that engaging with people in a positive way is life changing. This small group of intentional, positive relationship creators—or said differently, those who create intimacy—will be happier and more successful. They clearly look for new relationships and ways to go deeper into those relationships. This is the place we want to spend most of our time. If you can set yourself apart, be an intentional connector in people's lives, you will be an intimate adviser and reap all that is available to you.

STAY CURIOUS MY FRIEND

In Bob Dylan's classic song "Forever Young," the artist instructs us to stay young—young at heart, young at thought, and young at action.

FACE TO FACE

It occurred to me recently that this concept of youthfulness is a great notion to achieve success and significance in your practice today.

The truth that really penetrated my thoughts was the concept of staying curious. Like a child, always ask, "Why?" Always be interested. Continuously seek understanding. This trait will keep you young, but it will also open new ways of thinking, producing, selling, and living.

What occurred that refreshed my view of curiosity and staying young? It hit me while dragging the entire family—my wife, three teenagers, and our nine-year-old—out for a little frolicking fun. We traversed from the suburbs of Chicago down to the John G. Shedd Aquarium. Since the ticket line was long, I moved us up to the annual membership line and proceeded to purchase the family package. I rationalized that with just one more visit this year, the membership would pay for itself and we were doing a good thing to support the animals. Finally, I admitted to my son, the line was a lot shorter and I didn't want to waste time.

As new members, we were all handed our entrance bracelets for the day and tickets to a 12:30 p.m. show. Honestly, I didn't really listen to the lady when she explained what the show was.

About five minutes before the show was to start, I said to my family, "Let's go to this show." My three teenagers groaned and complained and, I confess, my wife and I weren't excited either. We looked at each other as if to say, "We don't want to sit and listen to some guy talk about fish."

It was my nine-year-old daughter that finally said, "Let's go! Why wouldn't we go? What is the show about, anyway?"

We all went in, albeit a few minutes late, dragging the teenagers behind the nine-year-old. To our surprise, we were all amazed. I'm not sure the last time you've been to a dolphin show, but this experience was like no other I had ever seen as a kid.

This was a modernized musical dolphin extravaganza. It included a three-story high multi-media screen "floating" on top of the water.

LISTEN AND LEARN

It included video shots of the dolphins and beluga whales in action, movie scenes of them in the wild, and multi-level screen shots of almost anything else that could create an emotional response as your eyes flipped from the screen to the real mammals doing amazing things in the water. The men and women in, on, and above the water were directing these creatures with stellar precision and grace—like acrobats in a circus. An accompanying acoustic guitar and singing trio added to the entertainment. This was not the dolphin show of my youth. It captured every sense and emotion possible.

What lesson did I learn? Lesson one was because the tickets were given to us for "free" we placed no value on them. Boy, were we were wrong. More importantly, lesson two was because of the curiosity of my daughter, we all enjoyed the show that just a moment earlier we had written off as an inconvenience at best.

What does this mean to you? Stay curious. Ask the *why* questions. Be child-like in your exploration of new ideas and experiences. We all were curious once, but somewhere between the demands of life, our obligations, and our commitments, we lost our sense of awe and wonder. The great news is we all have an innate ability to be curious. It's inside each of us and when turned on and tuned in, curiosity will lead to more success and significant relationships.

> ***Stay curious, ask the why questions***

Genuine curiosity will lead you to modernizing your own sales approach, creating an innovative solution, understanding your clients' needs and wants better, and learning even more about life and yourself. If you believe you've learned enough, you've stopped asking why.

So what can child-like curiosity do for you?

- Modernize your approach or your technique
- Open your mind to new ideas
- Help you learn
- Enjoy people more
- Keep you optimistic

FACE TO FACE

- Love life
- Be grateful

Those are the results that matter. Those are attributes that will change lives. Those features arrive because we stay curious and ask, "Why?"

Let me close this section with some youthful words from the not-so-youthful Mr. Dylan's benediction as you attempt to stay "Forever Young." (Lyrics by Bob Dylan, 1974)

> May your hands always be busy
> May your feet always be swift
> May you have a strong foundation
> When the winds of changes shift
> May your heart always be joyful
> And may your song always be sung
> May you stay forever young
> Forever young, forever young
> May you stay forever young

SET YOUR MAIN GOAL

What are you after? What are you thinking and pursuing when attracting clients? Below are some examples of what advisers might be thinking (in terms of goals) when attracting clients:

- I want to build my business. This client would be a valuable step in reaching that goal.
- This is a person of influence. If I can win this client, I will gain many referrals.
- I would love to manage this client's assets. It would be a welcome challenge.
- This client would be a trouble-free client. I would gain great benefit without big hassle.
- This client fits well into my business niche. We are a good match.

What do you notice about these very reasonable goals? They're all about what the client will give you and what you will gain from the client. The focus is on the object of the goal: larger business, referrals, the challenge, the reward, and compatibility with your practice. I'm not criticizing these types of goals. After all, this is a business relationship. In business, people are supposed to bring a benefit to the business partnership. You scratch my back and I'll scratch yours. There is absolutely nothing wrong with wanting positive objective benefits from clients. We are in business to profit; it's not a charitable service. For men, it is acceptable to want to win and gain a prize. Winning is expected and respected. What man does not admire the top producer in his profession (even grudgingly)? However, with women, you are on dangerous ground if gaining the object is your first goal. It will set your perspective and affect how you treat women clients, and it's risky. More on that later.

When it comes to goals, remember these three simple rules:

1. Your first goal is to build a strong relationship.
2. Your second goal is to never forget about the relationship.
3. Your third goal is to keep the relationship in mind as you do all the other important things.

BEING PRACTICAL AND INTENTIONAL

Putting your relationships first doesn't require a complicated multistep plan. If your strategy is not practical, it most likely will not be implemented. And when you do decide to execute a plan, think about your days ahead and prepare with intention and purpose. My friend and mentor, Robert D. Smith, tackled this topic in his book, *20,000 Days and Counting* (Thomas Nelson Publishers, 2012). In it he urges us to consider each day as precious. Most people, he suggests, sleepwalk through day-to-day life, passively letting time slip away. Unfortunately, the only thing that can usually wake people up to the intensity of life is impending death. But what if it didn't have to be that way? *20,000 Days* presents simple strategies and concepts that, once applied, will enable readers to be 100% present and intentional with every passing minute of every day, for the rest of their lives. Might that be powerful?

Perhaps the simplest way to be practical and intentional and create intimacy is in our approach with our clients.

FACE TO FACE

MANAGING CLIENT EXPECTATIONS LIKE A DENTIST
I like going to the dentist. Does that tell you all you need to know to stop reading? I usually find it relaxing and feel good that I've stayed abreast of my oral health. I recognize, however, and with great understanding, that most people do not like sitting in that narrow leather chair with a light in your eyes, fingers and instruments in your mouth, and the occasional request to spit. It is, at best, uncomfortable, and at worse, a paralyzing fear for some.

Have you asked the clients you serve how they feel about their annual (or semiannual) visit with you? Do they feel uncomfortable, frustrated, or even perhaps fearful of the encounter? Ask them; they will tell you.

Of course, we don't draw blood or use laughing gas or reek of latex, but the research says many clients find it unpleasant to meet with you or even trust you enough to give you more of their very emotional, real, and significant family wealth.

Perhaps the reason some of your clients won't take your call as often as you'd like or won't come in to see you or better yet, will not bring their spouse in with them, is similar to why some people don't go to the dentist—they hate the experience. It's uncomfortable and impersonal. It may be a bit painful at times. It's concerning and causes more thought and work for everyone involved.

We can all agree that semiannual visits and teeth cleanings are the best preventative action you can take to reduce tooth decay, gum disease, and now—the medical community tells us—heart disease. However, there are still people out there that will not go to the dentist. It's not the cost, because most employee plans include dental visits. It's the fact that they don't like the experience. They don't like it because of past experience. They don't like it because of their concern for the future. They simply are afraid.

If your clients and prospects don't like the experience of seeing you, how can you save them from themselves? How can you provide the excellent investment, wealth and legacy advice and service that you and I know will keep their portfolios clean, healthy and strong? I promise that's the last dental analogy.

Recently, however, I learned a valuable lesson from my dentist. As I sat in my dentist's chair and had an old filling replaced and a new crown put on, I noticed the dentist and the assistant did something new—or perhaps I had never paid attention to their process before.

As the 60-minute procedure took place, they told me everything they were doing, were going to do, why they were doing it and about how long it would take. In other words, they did not let me create a false fear or draw conclusions that most likely would not occur. They walked me through everything they knew would occur during my time of uncertainty and anxiousness.

Do you have clients who are uncertain and anxious about the markets, their portfolios, retirement, or their generational wealth? Do you have clients in real pain? The reality is, how you manage or don't manage that pain really will make all the difference. It will set you apart, good or bad.

So let's simply use this experience I had in the dentist chair to create or—in most cases for you—recreate a positive connection with the clients you serve to get them comfortable or dare I say, even enjoying this painful, uncertain experience in life. The more you do that, the more trusted you would be. Now that's noble.

Tell them what you are going to do, why you are going to do it, what they can expect and how long it will take. And then tell them again and again and again. Don't keep them in the dark or worse, don't argue with them that there is nothing to worry about or that there is no pain. There is real pain; accept that and manage it.

Walk them, face to face, through the intimate process of wealth building that you know so well and actually can deliver to them. You are the reassuring, proficient, caring professional that they need and want. Keep it simple. Communicate often and openly. Create intimacy.

ATTITUDE: YOU DON'T HAVE TO CALL YOUR CLIENTS

The wealth that you provide the next generation must be built, not just with intellect, but also with compassion, emotion, and intimacy. I again have learned the significance of this purposeful choice. So many times I would grumble about having to do this or that. Recently, I was taught a valuable lesson that immediately made me think of financial service clients. It's a subtle change of perspective that caused great liberation and optimism, and it's the concept that says the following: I don't have to do this; I get to do it.

Think about that for a moment. The reminder came as I, along with three other adult leaders, were preparing 12 high school students for a short-term mission trip to the Dominican Republic. It was a difficult trip. It was difficult for several reasons: the work was hard (built and poured a foundation for a new orphanage home); the environment and facilities were very basic; and we were with high school students. Yet our students were so excited to serve the orphans at the local orphanage. They felt privileged to be there. What a special trip. They created their theme for the trip. "We don't *have* to go to the DR, we *get* to go."

> *This is your chance to set yourself apart*

I know sometimes it is very difficult to wake up and do certain things each day. Sometimes we dread just one of our to-dos so much that it causes us to procrastinate the entire day. Numerous books have been written on the topic.

One of the toughest things to do is to contact clients that you either have bad news to share with, don't want to talk to, or simply may not like. Or sometimes you fear what tangent they may go off on or what new questions or challenges they may introduce. More than just saying, "I must call them today," how about considering saying, "I get to call them today." That's right, you don't have to call your client ever again; you *GET* to call your client today.

After all, this is your chance to set yourself apart, deliver on your noble calling, and build multigenerational wealth and trust with them. Not a bad reason to call. Perhaps we should look forward to the privilege of helping our clients do what they say they want to do.

It is said that baseball legend Ernie Banks coined the phrase, "Let's play two," a phrase he used every day there was a ball game to show his love for the game. It's worth noting that he played only day baseball in Wrigley Field (under the July and August heat) and he never won a championship with the Cubs. But then again, no one has since 1908.

When I first met Ernie, it was one of life's little surprises that just seem to occur if we are aware, conscious, and available. It came at a time that I had been pondering a concept I titled "regret minimization," which is doing those things in life that you think about but rarely, if ever, act on. That's when this meeting opportunity came to me. And as you will see, I acted.

Ernie came to a client meeting on a rooftop outside of Wrigley Field. Although I did not attend the business event, I was delighted in the stories that were shared with me about him. A week later, a colleague called me and said, "Hey, meet Ernie at eleven a.m. Tuesday." Without question, I did just that and for that opportunity, I am grateful.

When I met Ernie, what did I find? He was fresh with relevant, creative business ideas, energy and most of all, optimism. He talked about core principles, perseverance, history, family and loyalty. One of the reasons I wanted to meet with him, I hate to confess, was to see if this reputation of optimism that was older than I am was real. Or, I had thought, was it trumped up? Was it simply lore, legend, a sweet old story? "Let's play two" is a phrase every Chicago Cubs die-hard fan knows. It was, as legend has it, how Ernie greeted every baseball game he played. A kind of the "glass is half full" mentality. Was it real? I wanted to know.

I'm happy to report that this genuine optimism was real and still is. He is the real deal. His optimism, attitude, and legend were not a gimmick; it was part of his being. I walked away from the first meeting a better man for just spending three hours with him. That is a rare gift.

Do your clients feel that way after a meeting with you? Do mine? Why not? How can they? Do we crave a spirit of optimism, desire a view of the world that is liberating, need new perspective, and simply want to be better for knowing someone?

FACE TO FACE

I believe Ernie has another story to be told, not just that of his life, his baseball career, and his baseball success. He has many stories of perseverance, triumph, and pure joy. Those are the stories that truly last. This is what makes legacy. This is what needs to be honored and held up to the youth as an example of character.

After I met Ernie, another thought came into my mind, a thought I'm not proud of. I wondered quietly if he was thinking clearly. Yes, I am a cynic, but over time, life does this to you if you are not careful. The stresses of the world, the disappointments of people, the culture of bigger and better causes you to consider, look for, and find the negatives that may or may not truly exist.

After hearing him with great clarity and excitement share several business ideas with me, I had this urge to simply dismiss him. Discard the ideas not on their merits, but rather because they were coming from this old man. In reality, I thought, I was discarding him, not simply his ideas. I wondered if perhaps he was not thinking as clearly as someone half his age, who by society's standard would be a captain of commerce, a business leader. But a man of his age, early 80s, simply should be left behind to smile and rock. So goes the silent generation of today.

And then it hit me. Why would I think that? Have we as a society discarded the wit, wisdom, and wealth from our wisest and most experienced citizens? Do we think they are finished contributing? I sure hope not. This meeting was a great reminder for me, and perhaps hopefully you, that there are indeed powerful things still to learn, experience, and act on that come from the most treasured group of people on earth today—those who have lived long and lived well—the silent generation. These are the people who endured the Great Depression and World War II. They fought hard, worked diligently, and contributed to the glory of our nation. Many of these people are your clients. Listen and learn from them. Call them today.

Enjoy the game and begin believing again—believing in yourself and in other people. Think about it, you get to call your clients today. You sure are lucky.

Action Exercise: The true test of your brand is your clients' perspective. How do your clients and prospects perceive you? Whether through a one-on-one conversation, an e-mailed survey, or a phone survey, the following are suggested questions to ask your clients. Start with your top 10 clients and go from there.

1. What values/qualities come to mind when you think of me?
2. Why did you choose to work with me?
3. What makes me different from other wealth advisers you have worked with?
4. What would you tell a friend about me?

It's up to you whether you want to conduct the survey or have a third-party do it, just be sure to check with your compliance department to be sure you have proper approval.

Your business, the environment around you, and your life are ever changing. This state of chaos and confusion is opportunity knocking for those who embrace change. Three demographic fault lines exist today that, if navigated successfully, can catapult the intimate wealth adviser to new levels of success and production. That treacherous trip will only be successfully navigated by creating intimacy. The three key trends in our business today are:

- The Aging Population
- The Greatest Transfer of Wealth
- The Female Client

The next three chapters will focus on each of these trends, their implications in today's changing market, and what they mean to you, the intimate wealth adviser.

CHAPTER FOUR
THE AGING POPULATION

You know the data. It's all around us and becoming more relevant each day. Whether it's your business, the economy, the globe, or most significantly, your personal life, we all either know someone or are dealing with the ramifications ourselves of aging. What does this mean for us, society, and our planet? What does this mean for your practice, your clients? How do you serve an aging client? Consider this:

- 2/3 of all humans who ever lived on earth, and reached age 65, are alive today.
- Average American who retires at 65 lives for 18+ years.
- There is a lower savings rate, declining pension plans, weakened Social Security. (Source: Bureau of the Census)

These trends and so many others have an impact not just on you and your family, but on the clients you serve and their ability to create, protect, and transfer wealth and legacy. If you as their intimate wealth adviser do not identify and address these trends and concerns, who will? Who should?

For starters, this is you. Are you prepared? Is your business prepared? Do you have an exit strategy? According to TD Ameritrade, less than 30% of Registered Investment Advisers (RIA) have begun planning an exit for their practice, while the average age of the advisory business principle is 57 years old. Do you just do what you do for your clients without any consideration for your own wealth and legacy plan? I hope not. What do flight attendants say during their safety presentation before the plane takes off? In the event of an emergency, put on your oxygen mask first before helping others. Same thing goes in our industry. You can't teach what you don't know. You must have your own affairs in order before you can effectively influence your clients to do the same. It's absolutely unacceptable to think you can perform one way in business, while being incongruent in your personal life. Not with legacy. There's too much at stake.

Why is it that nearly half (46%) of financial planners say they have no retirement plan for themselves, according to a December 2013 Financial Planning Association (FPA) study. Respectfully, that is unacceptable. We must practice what we preach.

If the vast majority of the clients you serve are baby boomers, meaning they were born during the post-World War II baby boom between 1946 and 1964, ask yourself if you are prepared for the longest individual retirement period in history.

The longest individual retirement period ever comes from more wealth being created and more of us living longer after we retire. This trend brings challenges and opportunities. The old-school advisers say yes to this trend because it allows the professional adviser to manage that aging client's money even longer (and get paid to do so) or 18 more years of getting paid to do their taxes or update their trust and will. That is indeed true. But, for the new-age intimate wealth adviser, it also gives you the opportunity to really meet your aging client's day-to-day needs in a profound and intentional way, while also bringing value to the next generation.

SEASONS OF LIFE

Recently, a 46-year-old successful businesswoman shared this story with me. She and her husband have no children and both work and have a

THE AGING POPULATION

relationship with a financial professional for investments. Her husband liked the adviser, as did she. But her husband was content with the relationship amounting to an annual visit and quarterly performance reports. She, however, desired more. This became painfully obvious to her when she shared with this financial professional the fact that her mother was diagnosed with Alzheimer's disease. From that point on and for just over two years when her mother passed, this "trusted" financial investment professional "never once again asked how Mom was doing or is there anything he could do." This successful, married, 46-year-old businesswoman fired this adviser for "malpractice." And guess who supported her the most? Her husband.

You might cry outlier. Nope. This is very common. You might further say that the adviser was a bad, uncaring adviser. If I had a nickel for how many times I hear of that type of malpractice...you know the rest.

Is it your job to help her dear mother navigate through this difficult season of life? YES! You, the intimate wealth adviser, help them create and protect wealth. Why wouldn't you help transfer that wealth? Why wouldn't you help your aging clients in all aspects of their life, not just those that are about their portfolio or taxes or trust? You are her trusted adviser and her family's trusted adviser; you must help her, within your ability, on all aspects of her life, wealth, and legacy. That's what's at stake and that's where opportunity exists if you are a lifelong, multigenerational intimate wealth adviser bringing true value to the clients you serve.

We are all living in different seasons of life. It's your job to help your clients identify and accept where they are currently, plan for what's next and take precautionary steps should the unexpected occur.

Everything on earth has its own time and its own season

Different seasons can be marked by life events including accepting a new job, starting a family, buying a house, going through a divorce, funding a college education, recuperating from a health crisis, or settling an estate. It's critical for you to support your clients in getting and keeping their affairs in order as they transition from one life event to another. I've seen families scramble to locate important documents or passwords, especially during crisis. Do you have all of your important information in one spot? Have you encouraged your clients to do the same?

To support you with this task, please visit my website (www.3qadvisers.com) and download your free copy of our *Transitions Organizer*. It is a powerful tool that you can use to inventory and record all of your client's key documents and it's my gift to you. Take the time to fully complete it with your clients and review it annually and with each update.

What else can you do? What services can you provide to strengthen emotional intimacy? Get creative. Consider your service model and the network of experts and partners you work with and events you can deliver. We'll talk more about this in Chapter Seven, but one idea that I have seen work well is partnering up with any high-end assisted living facility in your community. Those organizations, which are big businesses set up for big results, have professional men and women on staff that would be willing to help you with your best clients (and prospects) to educate and equip your aging client base (and their mid-40-year-old children) on the key elements of helping Mom and Dad begin the difficult decision-making process of moving from their home into an assisted living facility.

If you were the one to facilitate that professional, educational meeting, would you be the one that reaps the benefits from both the aging client who is in need of considering that move, and their children, which may or may not be your client today?

Plus, I believe it is your job to not only build their wealth, but also to help them pass it on and live out their life in dignity as you help the next generation with one of the greatest love burdens they will experience. Now that's noble!

HOW CAN YOU SERVE?

I met a team of advisers in Greensboro, North Carolina, who understood how to meet the real needs of an aging client. They shared this story that wowed me. They had an affluent elderly couple whose husband had passed away. That couple lived in a "high-rent" part of the city. Think about the neighborhoods and cities that you serve. You know where the wealthy people live. So do, by the way, criminals. In that part of Greensboro, burglars were ripping off wealthy people's homes when, get this, the widow was at a funeral. Why? The criminal (that's a nice word for him) knew the house would be empty for four hours as dear old Widow Smith buried her dead husband. Nice. (You can't make this stuff up.)

These three advisers went to their affluent, recently widowed client and simply said they would house sit for her since they knew she was concerned at this time with the recent news of these crimes. So all they did that day from about nine thirty in the morning to two o'clock in the afternoon was sit in this woman's house, watching CNBC and making a few calls. They shared with me that initially they thought it was the biggest waste of time they had spent together.

Until what? Until Widow Smith came back home with her friends, family, and neighbors. Do you know that wealthy people hang out with wealthy people? These three advisers did not house sit for their client in her hour of need to get more clients, they did that rather because they simply wanted to help her—to meet her needs at this time in her life. But, because of that genuine act of intimacy, kindness, and service, they did get more clients and got further emotionally attached with other family members. Can you imagine what cousin Rose thought about this act, especially since her professional service providers didn't even send a card when she lost her husband?

Now that's noble and good business.

Get creative and think of ways to serve your aging clients and their families in a way that goes beyond just managing their money, their taxes, their insurance policies, or their will and trust. They and their children and grandchildren will be very grateful.

THE LEGACY CONVERSATION
Building lifelong, multigenerational relationships through meaningful legacy conversations is critical. Statistics can be daunting, but this may be one of the toughest actions or steps to take. Did you know that, according

to "Engaging and Retaining Families," *Investments & Wealth Monitor* (IMCA, September/October 2011), 98% of adult children switch financial advisers once they have received their inheritance from their parents?

This may be an appropriate moment for you to take the time to reflect on your own practice. Do you have a relationship with the next generation of your current client base? Will you be part of this statistic? Or will you be the one to break it? My hope for you is the latter.

The truth is we all know that conversations about money with family can be very difficult. Whether it's with elderly parents, adult children, young children, or grandchildren, the conversations are tough and in some families completely taboo.

Further research by Ameriprise Financial in 2012 called "Money Across Generations II" shows us that 55% of adult children feel they haven't had adequate conversations with their boomer parents about their financial situation.

How can you help your clients facilitate these conversations with greater ease? My suggestion is by becoming an intimate wealth adviser. Do you believe that if you could create that openness with your clients you would have a tremendously better relationship with them?

I know that conversations among the generations, especially about finances, can be a struggle. I believe that discussions with family may be easier when incorporating conversations around family values and core beliefs—in other words, the intangibles.

You, as the trusted, intimate wealth adviser, can be the one to introduce meaningful legacy conversations to your clients and their families. Women typically are the natural matriarchs to introduce these legacy conversations. As a matter of fact, women are more likely than men to initiate financial conversations with their families in general.

Our age and life experiences may vary, but remind your clients that every family member has a voice and can contribute wisdom.

THE AGING POPULATION

GETTING STARTED

A great way to get started introducing legacy conversations is to encourage your clients to arrange a family meal or meeting. Holidays in particular are ideal times for storytelling, talking about family traditions, culture, etc.

The sad truth is that rarely do we set aside time to talk about what really matters. Regrettably, I know this from experience. I'm pretty confident that my story is not unique—we all share a version of this story—whether you're a spouse, a parent, or a business owner. This story I'm going to share really is not about me, although my wife and kids have heard that line plenty. It's actually about you. It's also about your clients.

> **Women are more likely than men to initiate financial conversations with their families**

I come from a family of seven children, six guys one girl. My dad is Italian, my mother Irish. Are you concerned yet? My father's father, my grandpa, whose name was Rocco, came to the United States, like so many immigrants, in the early 1900s. I didn't know much about him; he died when I was in the fifth grade. I do remember when he visited us, we had to drive to Chicago and get him and my grandma because they never learned to drive. I also remember he did not speak that much English. When he visited us, he would wake up early and walk around the neighborhood, which no one in the suburbs did at that time. He would often sit in the garage door area on a lawn chair and smoke his pipe. And on rare occasions, he would tend to the garden in our yard.

My dad had one brother, a priest, also named Rocco. Therefore, I had no cousins on my dad's side. My dad grew up with five male cousins, his dad's brother's kids. They were contemporaries and lived in the same Chicago neighborhood and some even in the same brownstone apartment building. They were close. I knew those men a bit when I was growing up. I saw them at funerals and weddings, but I did not know their children, who did not live near us.

Fast forward many years, recently, through LinkedIn, I had dialogue with one of my dad's cousin's kids, who is 15 years younger than me and living near us. Long story short, we got all of my dad's cousins together, with some of their adult children and my siblings, and we had a wonderful family gathering—in the garage at my house—and the wine and stories flowed in large consumption. My children listened, especially my three daughters, with great enthusiasm, which surprised me. That day I learned that my grandpa Rocco first made that long and difficult journey to America at 14 years old with his older brothers. The other immigrants in Chicago immediately tried to put him to work in a factory, so his brothers, upon their mother's request, sent him back to the small village south of Naples, Italy. She wanted him to be educated. When he was 16 years old, she sent him back to America for good.

I also learned that my grandfather spent 41 years as a shoemaker. My dad's 77-year-old cousin told me that his Uncle Rocco had a permanent indentation on his chest from years of holding a shoe against his body while he applied the heel, for eight hours a day for 41 years. He also shared that he took three busses to get to that shoe factory. I was fascinated.

Besides giving me new insight to my heritage, it caused me to pause and ask why my dad never told me these kinds of stories. There is value in them. Regrettably, my dad has passed, as well as my mother, and those stories, facts, and their history have all passed away as well. Now don't get me wrong, I have plenty of joyful experiences, such as being with my dad moments before his death, eulogizing my mother at her funeral, and speaking to nearly 1,500 people at my 44-year-old brother's funeral, mostly high school students. Those are all special and profound memories to me.

Why do I tell you this? Is it to make you think we are the Chicago version of the Sopranos? Not at all. It's because those stories and many others are part of my legacy. I have finally learned that those experiences are important. I have begun to codify those stories so that either now or sometime in the future I can share those stories with my children and perhaps grandchildren so they know what's important to their mother and me, what we believe, and where we came from.

This stuff matters, and these conversations have long-lasting emotional impacts on the lives of your clients. Do I need to connect the dots here? It will add value to those critical relationships you have and want to keep.

I believe that our industry and you as a noble leader in this industry, with a wonderful burden of creating, protecting, and transferring wealth to the next generation, have the opportunity to also help codify the same with your clients' legacy.

The following are a few questions you can use with your clients to help them to get started having legacy conversations:

- How do you define legacy?
- What would you like to add to your family's legacy?
- What are your core family values or beliefs?
- What family tradition is most important to you and why?
- Who do you admire most in your family and why?
- Who taught you the most about money and why?
- What mistakes have you made, lessons have you learned?
- What is most important to you in life?
- What philanthropy is most important to your family and why?
- What has been and still is your dream or wish?
- 50 years from now, how do you want to be remembered?

BENEFITS TO YOUR BUSINESS

Going face to face and becoming an intimate wealth adviser and introducing legacy conversations will benefit your business in many ways. First and foremost, it will strengthen your tie to multiple generations by changing the client experience. Your clients will be grateful and loyal to you for life for the legacy you've helped them to pass on. Other advisers are not doing this, that's why only 2% of adult children are keeping their parents' adviser when their parents pass on. This concept will truly set you apart from your competitors, ultimately providing you more referrals and better relationships.

Action Exercise: Take the time right now to write down who of your current clients you will approach to initiate the legacy conversation. It is a fact that a goal written is far more likely to be achieved than one that is simply considered. It is important to reflect, consider options, and write down what's important to you so you can begin executing on those goals and tactics. When you set a deadline for a goal, it becomes real. Commit today.

I will introduce legacy conversations to the following three current clients in the next 30 days.

1. _____
2. _____
3. _____

You will only see these benefits of this goal if you take action. Connect with your aging client. Show them you are there to support them during this season of their life. They want to know their family will be protected and cared for by you, their intimate adviser.

CHAPTER FIVE
THE GREATEST TRANSFER OF WEALTH

In the last chapter, we talked about reaching out to and serving your aging client base—the large, aging baby boomer demographic—and helping them navigate sensitive topics such as the end-of-life and legacy plans for their elderly parents as well as beginning their own legacy conversation with their children, now in their 30s and 40s. That's three generations of wealth transfer right there, not to mention if their children have children, making it four generations...and the cycle continues.

Today we are in the midst of the single greatest transfer of wealth the world has ever seen. What does this mean to your business if you are an intimate wealth adviser? Let's take a look at recent research.

BABY BOOMERS AND BEYOND
According to a study published in 2010, authored by the *Center for Retirement Research at Boston College for the MetLife Mature Market Institute,* quantifies how much baby boomers can expect to inherit over their lifetimes and the distribution of receipts by household type. Their best estimate is that baby boomers will inherit $8.4 trillion. Of this amount, $2.4 trillion has already been received, while the remaining

$6.0 trillion is anticipated and, therefore, subject to significant uncertainty. The $8.4 trillion figure is based on 2007 data, which predates the economic crisis. The impact of the crisis is highly uncertain. Evidence from the previous market crash suggests little change as the economy recovers, but an alternative assumption is that prospective inheritances will fall proportionately with declining asset values, which would cause a drop of $800 billion or 13%.

They estimate that two-thirds of boomer households will receive some inheritance over their lifetimes, with a median amount of $64,000. Although the incidence of receipt increases with income, 50% or more of households in all income will eventually receive an inheritance. Among those receiving inheritances, high-wealth households can expect to receive substantially more—an average of $1.5 million for those in the top wealth decile compared with $27,000 for those in the bottom decile. However, inheritance receipts have a proportionately larger impact on the current wealth of low-wealth households.

Most boomers will receive their inheritances in late middle age, reflecting a pattern in which wealth passes from parents to children on the death of the surviving parent. To date, the overwhelming majority of the boomers' inheritances have been received from parents (63% of inheritances and 74% of dollars), with grandparents as the second most common source. Few boomers now have living grandparents, but the majority has at least one living parent.

While most transfers occur when parents or grandparents die and leave money to the younger generation, some transfers occur while the older generations are still alive. Including these, inter vivos gifts would increase our estimate of total past and prospective transfers to the baby boomers from $8.4 to $11.6 trillion.

But even within wealth deciles, the distribution of receipts is highly unequal, and the medians for the top and bottom deciles are $335,000 and $8,000, respectively. Though high-wealth households receive much larger inheritances in dollar terms, these amounts represent a smaller share of their wealth—22% for those in the top decile compared to 64%

for those in the second-to-bottom decile. Considering only past inheritances, the median amount received by Boomers by 2007—adjusted for inflation—is about the same as that received by the preceding 1927–1945 birth cohort at the same ages.

Regardless of the anticipated amount, any prospective inheritance is uncertain. Parents or grandparents who expect to leave a bequest may revise their plans based on fluctuations in their asset values. Or they may exhaust their wealth as a result of medical costs or long lifespans. In short, boomer households should not count on an anticipated inheritance to eliminate the need for increased retirement savings.

OK, so statistics aside, there is money in play. You did your job by creating, protecting, and transferring wealth, but what's at stake is the next generation—the boomers' children—will most likely find a new adviser to help them manage that wealth. Now do you see the opportunity? There is money in motion, yet as we discussed at the beginning of the book, the wealthy say they want more contact; they want to know you care. So while you spend time and money prospecting new clients each year, all you have to do is get your aging, happy, wealthy clients to help you create a trusted relationship with their children (or even grandchildren). Simple, but not easy and certainly will not happen for you unless you are intentional and become the intimate wealth adviser.

GENERATIONAL CONNECTION

I met a longtime top-producing wealth adviser in Wisconsin who told me one thing he does to connect with the next generation of his wealthy clients, in particular the grandchildren who are still in their early 20s or even late teens. He invites them to play golf. I know what you are thinking—I was as well. Golf? Come on, these days, I'm supposed to believe that an old-school business tactic like this is a valuable way to create intimacy and connect with the next generation? It was for him. Here is the difference.

He belonged to a well-known private club in his market that his clients enjoyed and was where they wanted to play. He would regularly invite his wealthy older clients to a round of golf. The catch: they had to invite their grandson or granddaughter to play with them and make up the foursome. Can you imagine that? Have you seen public golf courses these days? They are filled with young people. The sport is very popular. What this adviser really did was facilitate a special five-hour, face-to-face encounter with his best older, wealthy clients and their grandchildren. Could the wealthy client have done it himself? Perhaps. But what did this cost the adviser? What did it get him? A generational connection and good will.

Imagine the conversation at the course that morning. "Grandpa, who are we playing golf with today?" "Well, you will meet and be hosted by your grandmother's and my adviser. This is the man/woman who is working with us so that we might be able to pass on our wealth and legacy to you and your siblings." Wow. How do you think that young person feels now? More important, how do you think your wealthy, older client feels now? All you did was facilitate that important, human connection. Intimacy.

The younger generation is part of an interesting time in history. Technology has created opportunities for streaming communication and information 24/7, immediate feedback and instant gratification. Teenagers and young adults have access to resources that we never had. While they can find avenues of support, they can also wind up in trouble. Learning how to manage credit, avoid debt, and plan for the future has been an issue with kids for a long time. It's not new. But what is new is the constant availability of everything on the Internet (yes, you know you can get anything online) so there are more chances for kids to make mistakes. Handling finances is a struggle for anyone, but for college kids and young professionals, it's increasingly becoming an issue. There is a sense of entitlement today that didn't exist for baby boomers and definitely not the silent generation. Young people see wealth. They see riches. They see stuff. You, as the intimate wealth adviser, can play a vital role in mentoring these young adults. Show them the rewards of working hard, investing, and giving back. It's not too late to intervene and show them a path to abundance.

We are in the midst of the greatest transfer of wealth in history. If the intimate wealth adviser is not in play, they will miss this opportunity. This is your chance to identify clients with generational issues. Find out what's important, to whom and why. Create intimacy with your clients and the ones receiving the next generation of wealth. Encourage intergenerational events. Solve generational communication challenges and bridge gaps for your client and her family. This area is where you really want and need a strong network of related professional business associates that you can count on, and that can count on you. More on that to come.

HELPING FURTHER LEGACY

For those who have been living under a rock, the A&E channel's number one watched reality show, *Duck Dynasty*, is the most popular show on cable TV today. In a nutshell, the show is about a Louisiana bayou family living the American dream. They turned a backyard duck call business into a thriving, multigenerational, family-run business while staying true to both their family values and rugged outdoorsman lifestyle.

To give you an idea of its success, according to the *Washington Post* (2/28/2013), *Duck Dynasty* is now the number one rated nonfiction series on cable this year. The back-to-back episodes, which opened its third season, more than doubled the franchise's second-season launch.

If you've watched the show, you know it's the Robertson family "cast of characters" that keeps bringing people back to tune in. People are hooked on it. Why? Characters matters.

But why is *Duck Dynasty* <u>not</u> reality? The reason is because this family actually truly understands how to run a family-owned business. Unfortunately, many companies, particularly family-run businesses, don't ever hit the maximum potential they could or actually reduce growth when there is a generational change in focus or leadership.

Have you ever caught an episode of *Kitchen Nightmares*? Yes, it's another reality show (who knew we could learn so much from reality TV?) where celebrity chef Gordon Ramsey goes into failing restaurants and helps the owners turn things around. There is always a great deal of blood, sweat, and (mostly) tears, especially when the family dynamic is involved.

So many restaurants are family owned, and often they're multigenerational. You have grandpa in the kitchen, dad working the books, mom handling front of house, and the kids waiting tables. Unfortunately, there is always dysfunction. By the time Gordon gets there, the family is on the brink of losing the business, their livelihood, and their legacy. But because of his genuine approach and his proven, practical strategies based on years of experience running Michelin Star restaurants, he helps these families rediscover their purpose, communicate with each other, and participate in their own rescue. It's never easy, but it's worth it.

The good news for family-owned businesses and the advisers that desire to serve them is there are many good reasons to watch *Duck Dynasty* and to learn.

Crazy as it may sound, this show is a great example of thousands of prospective clients to you, if you are able to manage the family as they run the family business. You cannot separate the two. The Robertson family shows us that. This is a huge challenge for the adviser who is seeking to grow their business and serve this significant market place.

Consider the following: (according to Keenesaw University, Cox Family Enterprise Center)

- 80% of the world's businesses are family owned.
- Family run businesses account for more than half of the nation's gross domestic product.
- Nearly 35% of family-owned businesses are Fortune 500 and other large companies, including Ford, Koch Industries, Cargill, Wal-Mart, Weyerhaeuser, and Ikea.
- Approximately 60% of all public companies in the United States are family controlled.
- Family-owned businesses account for 60% of total US employment, 78% of all new jobs, and 65% of all wages paid.
- More than 25% of family firms expect the next CEO to be a woman.
- Only 30% of all family-owned businesses survive into the second generation.

What does this data tell us? It says there are billions of dollars in the hands of families that must learn to live together and work together.

What can the financial services industry learn from the Robertson family, as thousands of families like them take on the daily challenges of running a family business?

According to Chuck Meek, partner at Atticus Bailey, a consulting firm specializing in family-run business, "The key is to understand all forms of capital critical to the family business—financial, intellectual, social, and human." Meek adds if advisers can address those opportunities to the family, they will set themselves apart and earn their trust.

As you prospect, retain, and attract clients, particularly family-run businesses and business-owners, consider what they need to do and how you can equip them to do it better. Family-run businesses that care about culture, results, and process have a much better chance of achieving multigenerational success.

The Robertson family is good for business and to look at as a case study for the advisers that want to attract new clients that are family-owned and family-operated businesses. Duck Commander (the Robertson family business) poses three core principles that help them succeed as they have moved to the second generation of leadership and operations, a second generation that rivaled the first in terms of growth:

> Principle #1: Family (Generational Challenges, Legacy)
> Principle #2: Fun (Culture)
> Principle #3: Faith (Core Beliefs)

PRINCIPLE #1: FAMILY

The Robertson family does an awesome job at making sure there is a family transition plan. Each family member has their assigned roles and responsibilities, is held accountable, and understands their position on the team. The patriarch, Phil, understood this by not "giving" the company to one of his sons, but rather sold it. The children understand it by being allowed to make a decision to be part of the company, the same company that they saw firsthand growing up. All three generations now understand the power of transition and legacy. The young children know firsthand because they have been told what their grandparents did to start and grow this business. They all understand and respect leadership, particularly as it was transitioned.

As their adviser: Do you understand the family dynamics, and do you know if they have a transition plan?

PRINCIPLE #2: FUN
Watch the show and you will see what I mean; every episode is a new adventure. They have created a culture of fun. The Robertson family understands their culture, encourages it, and manages it. Strong, focused leadership and vision create culture. If those are poor, the culture is poor.

As their adviser: How have you added or distracted from their family culture?

PRINCIPLE #3: FAITH
Like culture, most family-run organizations have a strong faith story that may be worth sharing. The Robertson family makes no bones about their faith and how it affects the family business.

As their adviser: Have you asked the family-owned business leader who or what is important to them? What do they believe in? What faith stories have carried on for generations?

These principles are critical to the family and therefore are critical to you as the trusted adviser.

It's no secret that the Robertson family is brilliant at marketing, knows there is more to making and selling a product than the features and benefits of the product. Marketing and branding do matter. Creating a fun, exciting experience is key. And having a big vision is the difference maker. They have taken these elements to a level most companies' only dream about. They did it with a vision and a willingness to not let just one family member get all the credit and fame. They understand the importance of a team.

So as you look at your clients and consider prospects, consider who is running a family business and how deeply you are connected in that family's life, as well as the business. What can you do to help that family matriarch or patriarch create family generational wealth and legacy? Can you help them manage their business by providing related business resources and other specialized advisers such as CPAs, attorneys, and succession planning experts?

Perhaps you might also find resources for them that simply help the family, not just the business. Perhaps they desire help with literacy training, urban development, at-risk kids, or drug awareness. Maybe you can find resources for them that support educational desires they may have or help them create a foundation or an advisory board. Be creative and helpful. If you can become their intimate wealth adviser, you will serve them for years and perhaps you can help to make *Duck Dynasty* more of a reality.

Action Exercise: Creating multigenerational relationships are within your capability. All you have to do is pay attention to your clients when they talk to you about their family, their business, and their legacy. Find ways to engage other members of their family, whether in hosting events, educational seminars, or visiting their family business. Ask questions. Listen and learn. Resolve to make multigenerational relationships a priority in your practice.

I will conduct the following generational events in the next 90 days.

1. _____
2. _____
3. _____

As soon as you decide on what your first event will be, schedule it. Mark your calendar, tell your team, and move forward. Don't delay.

CHAPTER SIX
THE FEMALE CLIENT

My wife is the clear CFO in our family. It took us several years of marriage to figure this out, but she is the one who manages the money. Even though I have spent most of my career in financial services, Diane controls the checkbook. She is gifted with an eye for detail and is well organized. She also happens to be prudent and enjoys the responsibility more than me. We, of course, make investment decisions together and often discuss tactics, plans, and goals. But basically she controls the money flow, both short-term and long-term investments for our family.

Unfortunately, most people assume the opposite. Some would be highly embarrassed if they knew the error of their assumptions. For example, our family makes regular contributions to a particular missionary organization. Each year, my wife Diane writes, signs, and mails the check. Yet, I get a personal thank-you card annually addressed to me and written to me alone. We are grateful that a key leader takes the time to write a personal thank you; although, every year it's obvious that he believes I have written the check. At first it was humorous, but over the years it's become annoying.

SINS OF OMISSION AND COMMISSION

It's not just nonbusiness people who make these mistakes. I have had financial advisers, lawyers, and accountants send notes and cards just to me when they knew it was a joint account with Diane. These missteps are too common. As many female advisers I have spoken to told me, women clients who've had bad experiences with male advisers frequently approach them.

Because of this fact, some professional sales and service providers might be sadly mistaken if they continue to think that I (the man) make all the investment decisions. It's embarrassing for the sales professional, and I am convinced, in many cases, that it is unintentional. There certainly are sins of omission and sins of commission, but the bottom line is that ignorance can no longer cover this drastic oversight.

I'm here to tell you that my wife and I are not unique. The data is clear and getting stronger that the American female is currently controlling the assets both in the family and independently. It's not just purchasing power—we already know that to be true. But rather the investable assets she controls represent the majority of wealth in the United States for the first time. According to the Bureau of the Census, American women control 53% of all investable assets, which is roughly $14 trillion.

Moreover, today there are more women working than men and more women are graduating from US colleges than men. In addition, due to higher life expectancies for women over men and higher divorce rates, more single women are controlling wealth in their senior years than ever before.

What does this mean for you, the intimate wealth adviser? Perhaps more pointedly, what does it mean for the male wealth adviser? Today in the financial services industry, female advisers make up less than 20% of the registered professionals. I think it means we (as an industry) may need to change our game plan. Generally speaking (and I add with great caution to a delicate topic), male advisers either have not seen the data that supports this new world financial leader or don't know what to do about her—or perhaps both. If that's the case, this is your chance to understand the opportunity, challenges, and positive outcomes in store for you—that is if you can change old paradigms and prepare to genuinely and effectively serve the female client in a meaningful way. Perhaps it's time for a new perspective.

Consider this: women will inherit 70% of the $41 trillion in the intergenerational wealth transfer expected over the next 40 years. Source: Boston College Center on Wealth Philanthropy, 2009

Whether it is professional, educational, political, or with wealth, women control more than ever. In the US capitol, the executive boardroom, and the household, women finally have begun to find equilibrium. This demographic shift has turned into old news. The opportunity for the wealth adviser today is not simply to wake up and see what's happening, but more importantly, to figure out what you do about it.

In my first book, *The $14 Trillion Woman* (BookSurge, 2009), co-authored with Barbara Kay, we share some interesting data:

- For every 100 men that graduate from a US university, 133 women will graduate.
- Women still live longer than men, with the average age of widowhood being 56.
- 80–90% of women will be solely responsible for managing their own finances at some point in their life due to longer life expectancies and higher divorce rates.
- If a woman reaches her 50th birthday without cancer or heart disease, she can expect to reach age 92.
- 75% of women are single when they pass away.
- 75% of caretakers of elderly family members are women.

The female client—the numbers are just too big here. Ask yourself these questions: What does my business look like? Do I have many joint accounts that are male-centric? How many divorcees or widows do I work with? How many younger professional women am I engaged with? You must know your business and your clients in these terms.

Then ask yourself, generally speaking, who are better connectors? Who typically communicates more, shares stories more, and therefore is three times more likely to recommend a trusted service provider more? Who uses social media more? The number one users of social media are women between the ages of 35 and 55. The fastest growing segment on Facebook: women over 55, up 175.3%.

Facebook is growing faster with women than men in almost every age group. Women comprise 56.2% of Facebook's audience, up from 54.3%.

Source: http://www.insidefacebook.com/2009/02/02/fastest-growing-demographic-on-facebook-women-over-55/

Finally, who makes more decisions? Again, whether it's in a joint account or single, that data indicates women control the wealth and make more decisions about what service providers get used and which products ultimately get selected.

Working almost exclusively with the man in the joint accounts you manage is like creating a football game plan that focuses solely on assuming you have New England Patriots quarterback, Tom Brady. You may think you have created a winning financial wealth and life game plan to be in position to win with Brady (it certainly seems easy with him), but the fact is he will not even be in the game for the fourth and final quarter. You will have to win without Tom Brady. Why? Because Tom will be dead—statistically speaking. The quarterback of the family wealth in the final quarter will be Mrs. Brady, aka supermodel Gisele Bündchen, and you better hope that she thinks you care for her and have her best interests in mind. The data today indicates she doesn't believe that you do. As a matter of fact, she does not think our industry has her best interests in mind at all.

So, how can you rethink your strategy? From my book, *The $14 Trillion Woman,* here are three quick actions you can take now:

1. Change the language you use and the audiences you use it with. Speak straightforwardly and honestly to the female

client. Remove jargon. Address her, look her in the eyes, and watch your body language. Transparency builds trust.
2. Consider adding a female wealth professional or assistant to your team who may be better positioned to solicit the trust and confidence of the female client and prospect.
3. Spend time determining what specific female client/prospect you want to focus on. Is it the young professional? Divorcee? Widow? Senior? Be sure you have put the proper work into who your ideal female client is.

POWER OF PARTNERSHIP

Be open to the possibility that this opportunity, if addressed with seriousness and genuineness, may change your production forever.

In our business, we typically encounter the terms landing and retaining clients. These terms bring to mind the idea of capturing and owning a client, don't they? As if the client is an object for you to win. This terminology, which we are all guilty of using, sets the stage for a competitive approach. Men are frequently comfortable with a competitive approach. However, women are generally not.

When working with women, it's important to focus on cooperative equal partnership. This does not diminish your expertise or your value. Women come to advisers because they need professional knowledge and services. You can be the expert and work cooperatively at the same time in a relationship. You are not above them as a director, nor below them as a subordinate. Both you and the client have equally important roles. She is an expert in her life and what she wants financially. You are an expert on products and services to reach her goals.

Partnering with women clients is powerful for both the adviser and the client. The research shows us women are financial heavyweights. Equally important, they need you. Women have substantial financial needs, and they have been underserved for too long. You provide a tremendous opportunity to build their financial success.

So if you have a great deal of expertise to offer women and they want and need it, then why aren't they pounding down your door asking for your services? I'll tell you why. The biggest disconnection between women and financial services is the outdated and ineffective tactics used to earn female clients.

The traditional sales approach does not work well with women. Consumer research overwhelming confirms that women reject this approach. The old-school sales formula is rooted in the competitive model that focuses on capturing the sale.

> **The traditional sales approach does not work anymore**

Put on a good show and push for a commitment. It is all about showing attractiveness and winning. It has nothing to do with connection or partnering. It does not match a woman's way of relating. She doesn't want to be viewed as an object to be won or her money as a prize to be captured.

Even more, it does not match women's style of buying. In fact, it is so mismatched that a full third of women do not trust any salesperson—on principle. This research shows the competitive model of sales is not aligned with women's buying style. Here's how women buy:

- Consult their friends and people they know.
- Gather lots of information from many sources.
- Ask a lot of questions.
- Need/want time to consider.

When a woman tells a traditional salesperson they need more information, the salesperson will typically push to overcome the woman's hesitancy. They may interpret her hesitancy as stalling. If the woman then decides to think about it and revisit later, the traditional salesperson will push harder for commitment. The salesman fears loss of the sale if the customer walks out the door. Unfortunately, this method actually drives women away from the sale. It communicates to the woman that the salesperson is:

- Not listening to her.
- Wants to win the sale rather than help her.

THE FEMALE CLIENT

- Is not willing to answer questions cooperatively, is arguing with her.
- Is not working with her, is bulldozing her.

A friend told me a story of a sales technique gone terribly wrong. Her girlfriend was in Cabo San Lucas, Mexico, for a vacation and had accepted an invitation to visit a timeshare property. She actually did have some interest in perhaps purchasing a timeshare, as she loved Cabo and visited it at least once a year. The offer of a free dinner at a popular place in town just for sitting through the pitch didn't hurt either.

From the moment her friend stepped on the property, she was treated well, given complimentary breakfast, and escorted on a beautiful walking tour by a knowledgeable guide. Once back to the sales office, things took a turn for the worst. The friendly and considerate guide was replaced with an aggressive salesman who ushered her into a crowded room where other potential buyers were being pitched as well. He immediately put on the pressure for her friend to buy. When she told him that she absolutely would not be making such a big commitment that day, he chose not to hear her. She was very clear, but the man refused to relent. Finally, as her friend grew increasingly uncomfortable and distressed, she stood up and said in a voice loud enough for everyone else to hear that if he didn't accept her answer and let her leave, she would make a scene. With all eyes on him, the salesman gave up. Her friend hurried off the property, vowing never to return.

Of course, this is an extreme case of what can happen, but the fact is it does happen, even if it's subtler in its delivery. Bombarding a potential female client with calls and e-mails, using a confrontational or condescending tone in your communication, or creating a false sense of urgency will only turn her away.

If you've been frustrated when trying to secure women clients, perhaps the approach was the core problem. Prospects may be lost solely because of style. The key is to partner with (not capture) women clients.

HOW TO PARTNER WITH WOMEN

I learned the partnering model that I use in my practice from my friend and coauthor of *The $14 Trillion Woman*, Barbara Kay. She deserves the credit for teaching me this process that extends and expands the idea of connection all the way through the client relationship.

Barbara says there are five key areas to building a partnership: Connect, Understand, Integrate, Co-Create, and Serve.

Connect

Connection is the center of the partnering model. This is to remind everyone that you never leave that goal behind. Connecting, building, and preserving the relationship are central components throughout the life of the business partnership. Connecting rejects the traditional competitive model. As mentioned before, that model focuses on sales performance and the salesperson. This model shifts the focus to the client and building relationship with her.

Understand

The next stage in building a strong client relationship is the Understand phase. Reaching understanding is a process discussing (giving and getting information) and then coming to mutual conclusions by clarifying and confirming. This is patently obvious. It does not sound much different from any standard practice of working with clients. However, it's important that advisers appreciate the way most women do this process. It's different from the common practice of many men.

Integrate

Integration is the logical next step. You probably do this without thinking and it may seem unnecessary to explain; however, many women have gotten lost at this stage. While in the Understand phase, you were gathering what she wanted. Your role was facilitative. You actively listened and clarified her needs. In the Integrate phase, your part in the partnership becomes more proactive. This is the stage when you offer options and help the client understand choices. It's important to explain financial products in meaningful language. If you've been savvy during the Connect and Understand phases, you'll know if you can use financial jargon or whether you need to be more consumer-friendly.

Co-Create
During Co-Create you suggest the best options available and you work with her to create the best package for your overall business alliance.

Serve
Serve is to keep the relationship strong. In order to keep the relationship strong, you need to communicate and maintain trust.

Unlike traditional sales, this five-step model is not a linear equation. You don't conquer each step and then move on. This circular model emphasizes the continual focus on building and preserving the relationship.

THE POWER OF FEMALE VIRAL MARKETING

Earlier I posed the question: why aren't women clients pounding on your door? Ideally, you want these clients to seek you. That's viral marketing at its best.

Viral marketing is a relatively recent phenomenon that is fueled by social networks like YouTube, Twitter, and Facebook. We've all seen at least one silly cat video that has spread across multiple channels and received over one million views. Sometimes it happens by chance—a certain picture, article, or video resonates with someone who then passes it on to their network, and then it gets picked up by local media, where it catches the attention of a national news outlet. And from there it just takes off. Other times, it's more intentional and artists, advertisers, or aspiring stars create material and launch it under the purpose of getting their message or product into as many homes as possible. The goal is to get people to voluntarily seek it out, watch it, and share it with their networks. There is no end to how far it can go and viral marketing campaigns have become the standard for marketing and promotion.

The hook in most viral marketing is publicity stunts. This can be a very effective style of marketing, but women use relationship rather than publicity stunts or advertising as their resource. Since women value relationship, trust is a big factor for female consumers. Trust influences not only sales relationships but also product choices, but a history of selling instead of serving the customer may have soured women's trust in the sales relationship.

Women want every part of the purchasing process to be trustworthy. It avoids hassle. Much of the market research indicates that women today feel very pressed for time. They don't want to waste time or money. Untrustworthy products or services mean they have to spend more time and more money to get the job done.

Women want reliability whether they're seeking a product, service, or even a referral. That's why women use their personal relationships as referral sources, making it a two-way street. Women ask advice from other women and they also actively promote preferred services to their peers. They're confident a friend or family member will offer honest and trustworthy advice.

INSPIRING FEMALE VIRAL MARKETING

The female viral marketing network is already active and flowing. You don't have to make it from scratch or get it moving. It's there and running hot all the time. The key for intimate wealth advisers is to become accepted into the network and be positively promoted within it. It's equally important that you don't inadvertently join the negative network that runs alongside the promotion channel. Remember my friend's story from Cabo? Well, as soon as her friend returned home, besides telling everyone she knew about the awful experience, she also wrote a negative review for the timeshare property and shared it on more than one travel-advising website. She didn't want anyone to experience what she had endured.

When women network about products and services, they frequently give all their feedback into the woman-to-woman viral network. They don't just promote the positive providers, they also actively warn their peers against poor service. If another woman is present, the second woman will jump in with her own recommendations. If the women concur, then the force of the advice is magnified. The positive advertising is now strongly positive; likewise, the negative advertising is also reinforced. The power of both increases exponentially. The more a woman passes along toxic advertising, the more negative power it gains. Likewise, as positive referrals increase, the force of the promotion is strengthened. Women go to several sources, and the ultimate goal is to be a preferred adviser in multiple, overlapping female networks.

I have freelance clients in various areas of work—creative, health and wellness, business—whose projects or clients come solely from referrals, mostly from women. The best personal trainer, massage therapist, website designer, ghostwriter, marketing consultant, life coach, you name it—all you need to do is be part of the network.

LISTEN, SHOW INTEREST AND ASK
The first step in becoming a preferred adviser in female viral marketing networks is to remember the cardinal rule of working with women. It's all about the relationship.

Listen
Women promote those who have served them well and they do it spontaneously. Listen for service needs while you work with her. Also, listen for clues related to friends and family. Clues will probably come out in stories she tells. Pay close attention to the people mentioned and the needs you can fulfill.

Show Interest
Women are focused on trust in any relationship, so showing genuine interest (and action) in helping her builds trust. If you build trust, she will promote you. You can reach the next level by being invited into the network by asking questions and aligning yourself strategically with her network's interests.

Ask
The foundation of any invitation into her viral marketing network is a strong trust relationship. However, if you don't have confirmation of full satisfaction, verify that first. It will be a double negative if she's not fully satisfied and she thinks you're using her to get to her friends.

Once you've confirmed a strong bond, you can seek direct entry into her network. To your advantage, you provide a necessary life service. She regularly needs a financial adviser and so does everyone she knows. You can reach her network by offering to meet their needs.

Here are some examples of interest-gathering questions. Strategic questioning will provide important information, so show transparency and vulnerability when soliciting this type of honest feedback. The kind of conversation that will arise from these questions will increase trust and intimacy.

- My industry has not always met the needs of women well. Am I meeting your needs?
- What has been most helpful for you as we've worked together?
- I want to make sure that I serve you and others well. What kinds of concerns do you hear when you talk with your women friends?
- Financial services and products can be very complex. How can I help make this topic more accessible for your friends?
- What kind of outreach effort might be helpful to your friends and other women you know?
- People are so busy these days. I sure don't want to be an annoyance. What is the best way for someone like me to connect and offer my help?

These questions have the side benefit of eliciting important information about your service to her. If you're not already actively seeking her feedback, these will help you do it. As you ask these questions, be sure to listen for (verbal and nonverbal) cues about her receptivity. If she appears hesitant, in any way, quietly back off. When you feel resistance, it means you need to step back and build a higher level of trust.

In some cases a woman may be a strong advocate but not wish to invite you into her network with a direct introduction. She may prefer to just give friends your name, rather than invite you to a meeting or facilitate a personal connection. If that's her preference, go with it. Again, follow her cues.

A woman will communicate (either verbally or nonverbally) her level of willingness. It's just a matter of tuning in, listening, and showing genuine interest in helping her and her friends. She will guide you, if you take the time to listen. Remember if you serve her well, she will:

1. Be a loyal customer.
2. Refer you twice as often as male clients.
3. Recommend you three times as often as male clients.

You can receive all that even without being invited into her network. Imagine what you can do if she invites you in.

CONNECTION IS KEY ACROSS BOTH GENDERS

Most men and women connect differently. That's a given. Men's relationships tend to be task-focused and independent or connected around an activity or event. Communicating to create a personal bond is usually not the focus. When they do communicate, the interaction tends to be more competitive than cooperative. Even the best of friends will enjoy exchanging taunts.

Women do just the opposite. It's pretty clear that women are generally relationship-focused and cooperative. They connect by talking and sharing personal stories. As they interact they work to stay on an equal plane.

A competitive or cooperative relationship style is not better or worse; it's just different. We also need to remember that not every man and every woman fits the general tendency. There are men who are highly cooperative and relationship focused and women who are not. My goal is to make you aware of these general patterns, so you can have more insight into your own natural style and the styles of those around you. Take note of how the men in your environment relate. Also, note how the women tend to relate. The pattern will probably fit in general and, of course, there will be exceptions. It is important that you notice your own approach and become more adaptable to the perspective around you. If you find that the women around you and many women clients tend to have a cooperative style, it's important for you to shift to their perspective.

If you are used to managing clients and directing the sales/service process, then this is a big shift. If you tend to adapt yourself to your client's interests and personalize your approach to each person, the shift will be easier.

FACE TO FACE

Action Exercise: Men, before you approach female clients, think about the important women in other areas of your life and what they mean to you. Who is your strongest female relationship? Does she feel appreciated? How do you treat the women in your life—your mother, sister, business partner, your doctor, or your child's teacher? Remember, if you want to influence female clients, you need to be congruent in how you treat the rest of the women in your life. Let the women closest to you know that you care for them. Ask them for support and ideas as you begin your outreach to the female client.

I will connect with the following female prospects in the next 90 days.

1. _____
2. _____
3. _____

Female clients are valuable relationships. They offer a fresh perspective and a new challenge. Welcome them to your team, help them achieve their goals, and they will hold you near and dear to them for years to come.

CHAPTER SEVEN
YOUR COMPETITIVE ADVANTAGE

Teams are more important than ever. Whether you are part of a wirehouse financial service company, a registered investment adviser, a CPA firm, a law firm or a consulting organization that specializes in family offices, you most likely are part of a team. The power of teams has hit the wealth management industry. There are efficiencies and practicalities that make teams a reality.

Because of that, it is critical that the team is as functional as possible, focused on a mission, understands the value proposition, and works together for mutual results. This is not easy.

CHOOSE YOUR TEAM WISELY
One of the tremendous values a team offers is that it brings specialty service to your clients and introduces more prospecting opportunities to the team because of varied talents and connections. A strong communicator on a team adds tremendous value. No more so than the analytical type who spends much of his time behind the computer screen or the legal beagle who is constantly updating the team on the latest new tax scenarios or estate laws. Not only do all equip the team to manage the business

and the relationships better, there are those clients who simply are happier when they meet with or have an on-going relationship with someone other than the "client-facing" team member.

A larger, well-diverse team also offers you a much larger, well diverse network of professionals that each of you can tap into when need be. This too will help you maximize the return on investment and the return on human capital. This is another key area in your business to employ intimacy.

Several years ago I met and worked with a large team that managed $1.5 billion in assets under management. There were five people on this team: one analyst, two rainmakers, one operation expert, and finally one administrative assistant. They all played a key role in client meetings, prospecting and managing expectations. As a matter of fact, it came as a pleasant surprise to me when I heard the principle of the team (one of the self-proclaimed rainmakers) tell me that his analyst was responsible for finding and landing many of their clients. However, he said, it was his administrative assistant, who he claims was the real reason so many of their clients stayed with them. She was just simply magical in making their clients feel welcome, taken care of, and serviced on a daily bases.

He went on to share how she had been to numerous major client life-events on behalf of the team. Events like weddings, funerals, graduations, and family meetings. The administrative assistant was often times the face of the team. She was genuine, excellent at it, and trusted by many. Now that's valuable to the team.

How would you describe your team? Do you trust your administrative staff with your best, most affluent clients? The answer should be a resounding, yes! Be intentional about this. Invest in your team.

BUILDING A TEAM: BRONCO STYLE

A few years back, I had the privilege of delivering the introduction speech of a childhood friend as he was inducted into a local statewide sport hall of fame. It wasn't Canton, Ohio, but a privilege for me nonetheless. This friend had played six years in the NFL with the Denver

YOUR COMPETITIVE ADVANTAGE

Broncos and had started and played in three Super Bowls protecting the great Broncos quarterback, John Elway. He, however, was on the losing team each of those three Super Bowl games.

In his four years at a Big 10 university, he had the opportunity to start and play in three consecutive major NCAA bowl games—the Liberty Bowl, the Peach Bowl, and the granddaddy of them all, the Rose Bowl. He was on the losing team of each of those big games as well.

So it was with great pleasure that night to sit down with my wife, after I introduced him to the crowd, and listen to his humble speech of how he had all of that success. Interestingly enough, some people may not think that 0–6 in the biggest football games is success. But those people are mistaken and quite simply don't understand excellence and achievement.

He joked about his NCAA bowl failures and his NFL Super Bowl defeats. Then he looked down to our table, filled with his wife, three high school teammates, and their wives, and said, "Perhaps now you all know why all these years later I'm still sitting around with my high school buddies." He continued on to say, "Because that was my first and last championship team I played on." This was a reference to our 1981 high school undefeated 13-0 state championship football team.

I had not thought before in terms of both special memories and the unique bond that can occur when teammates have a shared vision and mutual success—even so many years later, despite ups and downs. A shared vision is powerful, fun, and enticing. It's a reminder to us that it's not just success that we are striving for, but more importantly, it's the ability to claim it with a special group of teammates.

In our industry and in our country today, we can all claim success and wealth. But can we claim being part of a successful team? And not only what that means professionally, but personally for all the team members? The by-products of a successful team cut through our day job and have ramifications in areas like our relationship with our spouse, children, community, and church.

Now more than ever in this fast-paced, ever changing, and difficult financial services business, we need to reconsider the art and concept of team. What does TEAM mean? How do we build one? How do we play on one? What is our vision?

Whether you are the head of a department, in charge of a team or currently part of a team the team concept cuts through your practice in a meaningful way. Equally importantly, it cuts through your relationships with your clients you serve in ways we need to take notice of—both positively and negatively.

In NFL coach Tony Dungy's book, *Quiet Strength* (Tyndale, 2007), we learn why ex-NFL players struggle in life in several key ways. Dungy asserts that the average ex-professional football player is far more likely than the population at large to battle with alcoholism, bankruptcy, divorce, and suicide. Why? Dungy says, in part, it's because they have lost their purpose and their group of like-minded partners who were in the huddle with them in good times and in bad. They, like all of us, need community to thrive. We desire it, we were made for it, and we are missing it. If six-foot-four, 300-pound, top-tier athletes need intimacy, why do we think we are any different. C'mon people!

In today's military for example, much attention is paid on re-acclimating veterans' post-war and helping them understand that they may not experience the same team-like mentality in the business and civilian world that they had in the foxhole. Fortunately, concerned citizens, activists, and fundraisers are answering the call to support the transition of these fearless men and women once they return home. An example is the Bob Woodruff Foundation, founded by its namesake, a US journalist who, while reporting in Iraq for ABC's "World News Tonight" in 2006, was seriously injured by a roadside bomb when it struck his vehicle. After a miraculous recovery, Bob made it his mission to give our injured heroes access to the high level of support and resources they deserve, for as long as they need it, by finding and funding innovative programs in communities where veterans, their families, and caregivers live and work. What's at stake? More than 2.5 million US service members have been deployed to Afghanistan and Iraq since September 11, 2001. About 1.5 million have returned; a million more are coming home. What's the opportunity? Let's ensure that their education and employment transition—and their future—is worthy of their sacrifice. Now that's noble.

You need team on the field. You need team at home. I'm not suggesting our lives are in jeopardy in the financial services business, but I am suggesting that teams that truly trust each other, care for each other, and support each other during good times and bad are far more likely to succeed and get results that are meaningful.

Building a sustainable team is important and difficult. It takes intentional efforts. Here are four simple factors to consider when building your team:

JUST LIVE

1. ***Leadership:*** A team needs to understand who is in charge. The leader needs to paint a clear, consistent vision of where the team is headed and what is expected by all of its members.

2. ***Inclusion:*** The leader needs to regularly include all team members in discussions, decisions and the results. Remember, not all things worth measuring count and not all things that you can count are worth measuring.

3. ***Vision:*** Each team member must clearly understand the team's vision, the goals, and even the strategies and tactics being implemented each day to obtain those goals.

4. ***Empathy:*** The team needs to have understanding and empathy with each other, recognizing that each team member has his/her strengths and weaknesses, good days, and bad days.

These four simple factors can help you articulate to your team what is important and repeat it often. It will put you in a better position to achieve something meaningful together.

FACE TO FACE

OK, let me tell you one more story about my buddy from high school. I know what you are thinking—get over the glory days. I respectfully say, make new glory days with old, simple truths.

On a crisp mid-October Friday night in 1981, we were playing our crosstown rivals at their stadium. The schools were only two and a half miles apart, so we dressed at our locker room and bused over. The buses dropped us off three blocks from the stadium. We put our helmets on and began to walk over, led by the 12-person drum core pounding on their drums. As we got closer to the stadium entrance, the student body of our rivals started to press up against us and force us against the exterior brick wall of the school's gymnasium, narrowing and blocking our path to the stadium. There was an estimated 8,000 people at that game—a very big number in those days.

My teammate, our all-American leader, who was leading us into the stadium, didn't appreciate the welcome we were getting and the fact that we were being prevented from doing what we had come to do. So our leader included us in his vision, with empathy for us, and led us that evening by physically clearing a path through rival students. It is even more comical today than it was at the moment, but sometimes your team and your clients need to know you are willing to remove obstacles that prevent them from reaching their goals—even if the obstacles are people. When he cleared that path, it gave the team a united feeling that someone was going to bat for us, that nothing was going to stand in our way, and that we were a lot more than a group of individuals—we were a team. Oh and by the way, the game was a donnybrook, but we won.

Knock down barriers to success for your teammates and clients. The results, and memories, may last a lifetime.

A NETWORK OF EXPERTISE

So you want clients knocking down your door, remember? But referrals are earned, not asked for. That's the new world order of asking for references from your best clients. It's insulting, annoying, and most do not appreciate it. However, when you add value to the life of the clients you serve, they will rave about you. They will tell their friends. Especially women, as we talked about, will highlight you within their network and all over social media. So earn referrals, don't ask for them.

Upgrading your services and the value proposition you offer is easy if you have a group of top professionals you trust and can count on in other areas of business that you can connect with and offer strategically to your best clients. Who wouldn't want help from an expert that comes highly recommended from another trusted expert?

> **Referrals are earned, not asked for**

Here are some typical examples of trusted professionals you should have in your network of experts:

- CPAs
- Estate Attorneys
- Corporate Attorneys
- Financial Planners
- Investment Managers
- Insurance Professionals
- Personal Bankers

Here are some other suggestions of professionals that may not be in your network, but perhaps should be. Remember, it's not just what they offer you; it's also what you offer them in a collaborative way to help each other grow your business and influence.

- Educators
- Social Media Experts
- Therapists
- Trainers (both corporate and wellness)
- Medical Professionals
- Assisted Living Professionals
- Succession Planning Consultants
- Investment Bankers
- Human Capital Professionals /HR Experts
- Life Coaches

If you can tap into other service providers, who are excellent and trustworthy, the opportunity to become even more indispensable and trusted with the clients you serve goes up. Your clients will appreciate all that you do for them, recommend you to their friends and family, and do more business with you.

Forging ties across different disciplines helps you stay in front of your clients at all times and allows you to be the first call. It is always fun and educational for you to learn from your peers of their disciplines as you grow your own practice and wealth. If you solve a problem for your best clients, even if that problem has nothing to do with their—fill in the blank: [Portfolio] [Taxes] [Trusts] [Insurance]—there is a far greater chance that those happy customers will refer you to their wealthy friends and family members. Again, referrals are earned, and this is a great way to earn them. Stop asking! Start showing your clients how valuable you are to them.

A few questions to ponder:

- Who do I know? Who knows me?
- What advocate do I need to connect to? How?
- Who can I add to my network?
- Why would this person want to connect with me?
- What value can I bring/services can I offer to my network?

THE ROLE OF TECHNOLOGY

Let's take a quick look at technology. Today, we have in our purse or on our belt, the greatest tool for disconnection—the smartphone. We have caller ID so we can easily now screen every call and decide to take it or not. We have e-mail, the web, texting, and social media. We shop online, compare online, critique online, and, at times, live online. All of these advancements are great, make no mistake, but each of them also puts new stress on our ability to have meaningful connection and intimacy. Remember the concept of listen and learn? Listening to connect is critical, but can become a major challenge when communicating electronically. E-mail, text, and other electronic avenues disburse data, but do not communicate feelings and intentions accurately; I don't care how many emoticons you use.

I recently had a painful reminder of this. I coach a sixth-grade girls' basketball team. I received an E-mail from a player's mother informing me that her daughter had a sprained ankle and would miss an upcoming practice. Intending to lighten the mood, I shot back a teasing e-mail, writing: "She'll be fine. Put some tape on it and get her to the game. There's no crying in basketball." Regrettably, the mother did not know my sense of humor and replied with a distressed e-mail insisting that her daughter was too injured to practice. I immediately called to clear up the misunderstanding and apologize.

> **When we mess up, fess up**

E-mail, texting, words, inflection, facial expression, and body language need to present a unified message for clear understanding. If any part of the communication is contradictory or missing, problems arise. We need to attend to our total communication picture in all its forms.

Let's consider the following facts:

- Facebook has grown in relatively a short time to over one billion users.
- 1/8 married couples met online.
- Over 87.8 billion monthly worldwide searches conducted on Google sites.
- Mobile Internet devices will outnumber humans this year.

Sources: 1. *Business Week*, October 04, 2012; 2. McKinsey Study, 2006; 3. Jeffbullas.com; 4. www.theguardian.com/technology/2013/feb/07

And as you read this, these data points are probably outdated. Things are changing quickly.

We must learn how to create intimacy in an ever-changing technological world. Technology is not bad; it just has made connecting and creating intimacy with others very different than it was just a few years ago. Luckily, through innovations like Skype, FaceTime, Google Hangout, and the like, we're able to use technology and communicate in real time without hiding behind a keyboard. It's not perfect, but it's certainly on the right track.

Action Exercise: When we think about team, we think outside of ourselves. We care about the other members, look out for them, and defend them when necessary. Evaluate your current professional team and your network of partners. Where are you strong? Where do you need reinforcement? Where can you expand?

I will add the following talent to my team in the next 12 months.

1. _____
2. _____
3. _____

I will connect to three new network business partners in the next 90 days

1. _____
2. _____
3. _____

Your team is an extension of you, your purpose, and your vision. Choose wisely.

CHAPTER EIGHT

SET YOURSELF APART

Today's intimate wealth adviser is faced with a difficult job—creating generational wealth, gaining trust, running an effective practice and balancing it all. For the professional who can do all of those things, there is no end to the good you can do and the wealth you can create.

I fully agree that your understanding of complex investment products, tax laws, insurance opportunities, and estate challenges are of critical importance. There are many wealth professionals that are technically proficient. So what separates you from the pack? I know, some of you are saying that your technical proficiency is what separates you from your competition. I'm sure you are smart and I'm sure you understand your product offerings. My point is, shouldn't every wealth adviser have a high level of technical expertise? Isn't that a standard job requirement? I'm not sure it's enough to separate you from the thousands of other advisers out there. And of course, for those who simply are not technically proficient, do us all a favor—go sell cars. You have an obligation to be technically proficient.

Knowledge and information are commodities. Your clients and prospects can get information from all sorts of sources today—some better than others and most are quicker than you. What they can't get is wisdom and intimacy.

I believe that relationships trump everything, and your ability to build trust comes from a simple formula—people need to like you and to trust you, and when they trust you, they will give you what you ask of them. You don't build trust by knowing the latest and greatest innovative investment solution, tax law or estate law change only. You do it by taking away a client's pain. You get it by building intimacy, which at its essence is trust.

START AT HOME

Building trust with your clients starts with how you create, appreciate, and manage wealth in your own home. My children look at Diane and me as a team. They already see their mother as knowledgeable, capable, and powerful when it comes to running the family finances. They see me as a willing partner, supporting and discussing our future plans, projects, and legacy. They see us falter, recover, and most of all, they hear our conversations so they, too, can learn how to manage themselves and their decisions.

When I bought an extravagant impulse purchase for the lake house not too long ago, Diane wasn't happy. The whole thing became a family topic and my oldest daughter teased me, "I can't believe you did that without telling Mom. You're in trouble." We all laughed. Instead of becoming a heavy and heated discussion, we kept it light, even though we all knew it was an expensive mistake. There are times to have serious conversations, but that wasn't one of them. I want my kids to appreciate what we have, trust that I'm here to protect them, but also know that it's OK to live and learn. No taboos about money here. I emphasize the long-term perspective and patience when it comes to building and managing wealth. In my family, I hope to instill the pursuit of joy, not money. That's my legacy. I want to be remembered as a great husband, father, and teacher. It's personal for me. It starts in my own home, continues on to my professional team and clients, and then on to the rest of the world.

What is your legacy? What do you stand for? Do you have the trust of your family, peers, colleagues, and clients? What will you do differently, starting today?

EXPAND YOUR REACH

Extending your knowledge and expertise beyond your home and client base will not only set you apart, it will transform you. I challenge you to step outside of yourself and your comfort zone and really stretch past what you know—or think you know—to create intimacy on a grand scale. When I embarked on this journey back in 2008, I had no idea it would lead me to one of my most profound experiences to date.

For one hour, every Tuesday morning for two semesters, I volunteered and taught a senior economics class at an urban, Christian college and life preparatory high school on Chicago's Near West side. This opportunity did not happen by chance, although it felt like it at the time, but it was completely in line with the path I was on personally, professionally, and spiritually.

I first met the headmaster, Bob, two years before when our company volunteered for a service project to support the building of what is now the Chicago Hope Academy (www.ChicagoHopeAcademy.org). We facilitated three consecutive Fridays during the summer of 2006 and were also there to celebrate the official opening in September. Our staff rallied around the cause, and it was a great start to the creation of our own corporate culture. I stayed in touch with Bob and supported the school monetarily during those early years.

Fast forward to 2008, Bob approached me one day and said, "Tony, I love and appreciate your money. But I want your hands and your heart. Come serve with me." I was honored, but I recall saying, "I've never taught. I don't know how." He answered, "Tony, they don't care. Just come and love them and teach them." And just like that, I did. That fall I stepped in and faced 17 high school seniors and embarked on an eye-opening, life-changing journey. It sounds cliché, but those kids taught me more than I ever could have taught them. In a community where reaching the age of 21 is considered old, I worked with students who were excited, smart, and ready to take on the challenges of the world.

I still consider my time in the classroom one of my greatest contributions to strengthening connection and relationships. What is it for you? What do you care about? How do you give back? When Diane and I tithe, especially on the rare occasions when we've given not out of abundance, but when it was harder to give, I saw it come back in spades. Not monetarily, but the overwhelming feeling of goodness that comes along with it. I can't put it into words, but my hope for you is that you get to experience it. Give what you have and even what you may not have. Trust that there is a bigger plan for you. Start with you and then spread your time, resources, and skills with your family, your community, and ultimately, your world.

So as you continue to build your trusted brand, grow your practice, and balance it all, consider these five critical questions to help you be the noble, dynamic, trusted adviser that you are.

FIVE CRITICAL QUESTIONS

1. Do you have a plan to become a consistent top-tier producer, or once again, remain one? One thing I've noticed that all top producers have in common is a plan and their commitment to that plan. You must remain open-minded but committed to your purpose and plan.

2. Will you be able to work less 10 years from now while earning more income and potentially generating greater generational wealth for your clients? Is your practice efficient, not just for your sake, but also for your client's sake? Are you able to serve them well, build generational wealth for them and yourself, and balance it all? If so, you are a better partner and adviser for them, and you will be rewarded for your value proposition.

3. How do you add value to your current client relationships? Or, what business are you in today: transaction, fee, or service? This question is all about adding value to build relationships in your book of business. I've seen top producers wrestle with these questions for years now and have found that all three aspects are important. Are you setting up your value proposition as an adviser today

to address these topics? If your business is geared on transactions, it may not withstand tough times and an aging, smarter client base. If your business is fee only, are you in a position to best serve your clients and yourself? I believe we are all in the service business—we must serve others to bring value, live out our purpose, and grow our business. Semantics? I don't think so.

4. Are you (and subsequently, your clients) aware of the risk to which your book (their portfolio) is exposed? This again is a question that causes you to consider both your technical proficiency and your bedside manner. Both are critical. If you don't have a service model and a solution offering that is transparent and easy to understand, enlightened clients and prospects will expose you in tough times.

5. Do you have a system in place to limit the number of positions you have in your practice, to a number that you can be held accountable to? The average $300,000 US producer had 1,100 individual securities in his/her book. That's ineffective. Again, have a simple, transparent plan, purpose, and offerings.

My goal is to help us rethink the success metrics in this business today and create a better sense of intimacy with our clients. By asking ourselves questions like this, we can gain a new perspective, create a greater purpose, and grow our influence and business accordingly. And when did a little self-assessment ever hurt us?

Find your own critical questions for your business today and continue to ask yourself those questions until you have the answers you desire.

In closing, this is hard work. But it is worth it, just like creating lifelong and multigenerational wealth is worth it. Remember, you are in the midst of a noble calling. So what is the final call to action here? I've shared stories and resources throughout the book. As I said, it is my hope that one or two of these resources are helpful to you in changing behaviors and growing your influence in the lives of the clients you serve. My hope is that you will lead the charge, set the standard, and make intimacy a core value in all of your business relationships, transactions and practices. One shift in your behavior, one change in perspective, and one kind act can have transformational results.

With that said, I'd like to leave you with a story from my friend and bestselling author Andy Andrews's book, *The Butterfly Effect* (Thomas Nelson/Simple Truths, 2009). May it inspire you to capture and preserve the stories of life and legacy for the families you serve. They will be grateful.

THE BUTTERFLY EFFECT

In 1963, Edward Lorenz presented a hypothesis to the New York Academy of Science. His theory, stated simply, was that:

A butterfly could flap its wings and set molecules of air in motion, which would move other molecules of air, in turn moving more molecules of air—eventually capable of starting a hurricane on the other side of the planet.

Lorenz and his ideas were literally laughed out of the conference. What he had proposed was ridiculous. It was preposterous. But it was fascinating!

Therefore, because of the idea's charm and intrigue, the so-called "butterfly effect" became a staple of science fiction, remaining for decades a combination of myth and legend spread only by comic books and bad movies.

So imagine the scientific community's shock and surprise when, more than 30 years after the possibility was introduced, physics professors working from colleges and universities worldwide came to the conclusion that the butterfly effect was authentic, accurate, and viable.

Soon after, it was accorded the status of a "law." Now known as The Law of Sensitive Dependence Upon Initial Conditions, this principle has proven to be a force encompassing more than mere butterfly wings. Science has shown the butterfly effect to engage with the first movement of any form of matter—including people.

On Friday, April 2, 2004, ABC News honored a man who, at that time, was 91 years old. The news program was running a regular segment called "Person of the Week." Usually the honoree's accomplishments are listed in advance and by the time the name is announced, most folks have already guessed the identity of that week's recipient. In this instance, however, the pronouncement left many viewers puzzled.

"And so...our Person of the Week is..." the anchorman finally said, "Norman Borlaug!"

One can only imagine the frowns. Who? Who did he say? Norman...what was the last name?

Yet, despite our unfamiliarity, Norman Borlaug is a man who is personally responsible for drastically and dramatically changing the world in which we live. You see, in the early 1940s, Norman Borlaug hybridized high-yield, disease-resistant corn and wheat for arid climates. From the dust bowl of Western Africa to our own desert Southwest, from South and Central America to the plains of Siberia, across Europe and Asia, Borlaug's specific seed product flourished and regenerated where no seed had ever thrived before. Through the years, it has now been calculated that Norman Borlaug's work saved more than two billion lives from famine.

Actually, it was never reported, but the anchorman was misinformed. It was not Norman Borlaug who saved the two billion people, though very few caught the mistake. It was Henry Wallace.

Henry Wallace was the vice president of the United States under Franklin Roosevelt. Over his four terms, Roosevelt had three different vice presidents, and the second man to serve was Henry Wallace.

Wallace was the former secretary of agriculture who, after his one term as vice president, was dumped from the ticket in favor of Truman. While

Wallace was vice president, however, he used the power of that office to create a station in Mexico whose sole purpose was to hybridize corn and wheat for arid climates. He hired a young man named Norman Borlaug to run it.

So Norman Borlaug won the Nobel Prize. And Norman Borlaug was awarded the Presidential Medal of Freedom. But considering the connection, it was really Henry Wallace that saved two billion people!

Or was it George Washington Carver? You remember Carver, don't you? The peanut?

But here's something that very few people know: When Carver was 19 years old and a student at Iowa State University, he had a dairy sciences professor who, on Saturday and Sunday afternoons, would allow his six-year-old boy to go on "botanical expeditions" with the brilliant student.

It was George Washington Carver who took that boy and instilled in him a love for plants and a vision for what they could do for humanity. It was George Washington Carver who pointed six-year-old Henry Wallace's life in a specific direction—long before he ever became vice president of the United States.

It's amazing to contemplate, isn't it?

George Washington Carver flapping his butterfly wings with the peanut. There are currently 266 things he developed from the peanut that we still use today. He flapped his wings with the sweet potato. There are 88 things Carver originated from the sweet potato that we still use today. And while no one was even looking, George Washington Carver flapped his wings a couple of times with a six-year-old boy. And just happened to save the lives of more than two billion people...and counting.

So maybe it should have been George Washington Carver—Person of the Week! Or the farmer from Diamond, Missouri?

His name was Moses and he lived in a slave state, but he didn't believe in slavery. This made him a target for psychopaths like Quantrill's Raiders who terrorized the area by destroying property by burning and killing. And sure enough, one cold January night, Quantrill's Raiders rode through Moses's farm. The outlaws burned the barn, shot several people, and dragged off a woman named Mary Washington who refused to let go of her infant son, George.

Now, Mary Washington was a friend of Moses's wife, Susan. Though distraught, Susan promptly set to work writing messages and contacting nearby farms. She got word through neighbors and towns and two days later managed to secure a meeting for Moses with the bandits.

Susan looked on anxiously as her husband rode off on a black horse. His destination was a crossroad in Kansas several hours to the north. There, at the appointed time, in the middle of the night, Moses met up with four of Quantrill's Raiders. They were on horseback, carrying torches, and had flour sacks tied over their heads with holes cut out for their eyes. There, the farmer traded the only horse they had left on their farm for what the outlaws threw him in a dirty burlap bag.

As the bandits thundered off on their horses, Moses fell to his knees and there, alone on that dark winter night, the farmer pulled from the bag a cold, naked, almost-dead baby boy. Quickly he jerked open his own coat and his shirt and placed the child next to his skin. Covering him with his own clothes and relying on the warmth from his own body, the man turned and walked that baby home.

Moses walked through the night and into the next morning to get the child to Susan. There, they committed to that tiny human being—and to each other—that they would care for him. They promised the boy an education to honor his mother, Mary, whom they knew was already dead. That night, they gave the baby their own name...and that is how Moses and Susan Carver came to raise that little baby, George Washington.

FACE TO FACE

So when you think about it, maybe it was the farmer from Diamond, Missouri, who saved the two billion people. Or was it his wife who was responsible? Certainly it was Susan who organized the effort—it was she who demanded immediate action.

Unless...

Create your legacy now. You will not regret doing so.

AFTERWORD

So what does this mean to you? Let me summarize. How do you create intimacy by creating purpose and community in your life and in your business? And how does this intimacy create lifelong and multigenerational clients? By going face to face with the most important people in your life.

Let me pose five simple ways to begin to consider moving more face to face. If it's not simple, it becomes more difficult for us to implement. Furthermore, one of the great lies of development is it has to be complicated to be true. I disagree. Therefore, I encourage you to consider the following.

Create community. Be intentional and practical, but figure out how to create community in your business, your family, with your friends, and even in your neighborhood. Sound simple? Is it?

Five ways to create community:

1. Community requires commitment
2. Community requires honesty
3. Community requires politeness
4. Community requires confidentiality
5. Community requires volume

Creating a close, productive community takes you to be committed to relationships—to the work associated with relationships, even when they are difficult. Which relationships usually are. People are not perfect, nor are you. Despite that, we must commit to cultivating a community for all the right reasons.

Community takes honesty. We must speak the truth with love. Not addressing conflict causes a lack of community. Addressing conflict may be the best way to create community. Resolution helps. Most of us need to have more patience and a gentler spirit when we deal with humans. Don't we require that from others when dealing with us? Be honest with our relationships, even when we look stupid. And, be honest with ourselves.

Creating community requires politeness. How often has our temper wreaked havoc on our community? Next time, think, slow down, and respond in a more professional and polite way—even if you were wronged. Take the proverbial high road; it may make all the difference for your well-being, as well as your business. The freedom of speech does not mean we always have to give our opinion. I confess, this one is very hard for me.

Community requires confidentiality. That's where trust grows from. People need a confidant, a trusted friend, and adviser. People desire one. We need someone who we can go to in our moments of weakness and despair. Who would become vulnerable to someone if they believed their secrets and fears would be shared? Would you accept that in your closest relationships? Why should your community accept lose lips, gossiping, and a lack of trust in theirs?

Creating community takes volume. You cannot have a relationship without proximity. The world has created a dangerous lie—quality time over quantity of time. All great, meaningful relationships require time together. That's how we were made. That's when we are at our best. For us to think we can have a strong, intimate, honest, and respectful community without investing our time into it is silly.

So, how do you become an intimate wealth adviser so you can create lifelong and multigenerational relationships? Invest in your community by being committed to it; by being honest with yourself and your community members, expand your politeness, professionalism, and genuine concern for others; commit to being confidential in those communities to better serve others and finally be frequently involved in those communities. The results will be life changing, and you will be a noble intimate wealth adviser.

Consider the simple, but not easy tactic of going face to face more often in your business today. All the best to you, in your difficult, but rewarding calling of creating lifelong and multigenerational wealth, legacy and relationships. You sure are lucky.

ADVANCED PRAISE FOR FACE TO FACE

"Finally we have a manual that spells it out for advisers seeking not only career success but life satisfaction. Whether you are starting out or starting over, *Face to Face* is a wonderful guidebook you will keep and refer to again and again."

>Candace Bahr, CDFA
>Co-founder, The Women's Institute for Financial Education (Wife.org) Registered & Principal, LPL Financial/ Bahr Investment Group

"*Face to Face* represents a simple, but powerful concept; by meeting the basic human psychological needs of others, or said differently, by having genuine connection with others, we are more productive, innovative, profitable, and trusting. If that is a list of attributes that you desire for yourself, for your clients, and for your friends and colleagues, then read this book."

>Tim Ursiny PhD, RCC, CBC
>Founder, Advantage Coaching & Training
>Author of *The Top Performer's Guide to Attitude* and *The Coward's Guide to Conflict*

"In a high-tech, computerized communication world, Tony's latest book helps advisers learn to genuinely connect with their clients on a new level...*Face to Face* is a roadmap to those meaningful relationships."

>Josh Gerry
>Senior Regional Vice President, AXA Distributors

"*Face to Face* is for any sales and service professional in any industry. These simple truths will help you grow your business."

>Paul Negris
>Regional Sales Manager, OxyChem subsidiary of Occidental Petroleum Corporation

FACE TO FACE

"Knowledge is derived by asking good questions. Tony offers thought provoking questions that allow the adviser to learn valuable insight into one's belief systems and business practices. Perhaps the questions asked will help your clients, and you, live more fulfilling, meaningful, and successful lives."

>J.D. Joyce, Author, *The Story of Rich*

"Most business and investment situations ignore long tern relationships, much less intimacy, values, happiness, and beliefs. When these factors are introduced, the process is enriched and becomes personal and enjoyable. *Face to Face* focuses on the process and benefits of including these and other personal relationship building concepts in our daily business and investment activity."

>Jim Hofner, CPA

"*Face To Face* really applies meaty, traditional principles into practical, new-age ways of being intentional about relationships that will make a difference in your practice and in your life. It will do the following: boost morale; increase productivity; retain assets, contracts and satisfied customers."

>Tom Powell, ESQ
>Partner, Powell and Boyer

"Great read! *Face to Face* graciously illuminates the importance of genuinely being interested in people. It is an enlightening reminder that success is a byproduct of serving our clients and having a vested interest in their lives and legacy. You will want copies to share with others!"

>Robin Westrom-Tardy
>Regional Vice President, Guggenheim Investments

ADVANCED PRAISE FOR FACE TO FACE

"It's been my pleasure to work with Tony. He is passionate and committed to helping others. Tony's care and authenticity shines through in all his relationships. Read *Face to Face* and gain from Tony's experience."

>Barbara Kay
>President Barbara Kay Coaching

"The beauty of *Face to Face* is Tony's ability to deconstruct a knotty problem and reconstruct it in a simpler form. Rather than drawing a map through the thicket, he hacks away at the brambles and shines light on a path leading to...two chairs."

>Chuck Meek, Owner
>Atticus Bailey, LLC

ABOUT THE AUTHOR

Tony DiLeonardi

As the founder of Third Quarter Advisers, Tony channels more than 25 years of sales and managerial experience to help inspire and guide wealth professionals through the challenges of running a dynamic wealth management practice. Third Quarter Advisers offers strategic best practices and coaching services and solutions for wealth advisers and their clients. Tony speaks regularly at meetings across North America and strives to equip attendees with the knowledge, skills and creative thinking needed for enhancing their overall businesses and personal lives.

Previously, he was vice chairman at Guggenheim Investments and at Claymore Securities, an exchange-traded fund specialist that was acquired by Guggenheim Partners.

Tony co-authored the book *The $14 Trillion Woman*. He earned a bachelor's degree in communications from Illinois State University. He lives with his wife and their four children near Chicago.

THIRD QUARTER ADVISERS
Third Quarter Advisers is an organization committed to serving the wealth professional who is seeking to be the trusted adviser to the affluent client as they create, protect, and transfer wealth and legacy for the clients they serve. Third Quarter Advisers does this by identifying and enhancing Purpose, Passion, Perspective, and Performance in the life of the trusted wealth adviser and distributes relevant content, coaching, and community to assist the wealth professional in building a more productive business, deeper relationships, and a more efficient practice.

FACE TO FACE

Proceeds from this book will support Chicago Hope Academy. Chicago Hope Academy is a co-educational, non-denominational college and life preparatory school dedicated to nurturing and challenging the whole person, mind, body and spirit, to the glory of God

You can learn more about it or support their efforts by visiting www.chicagohopeacademy.org

(312) 491-1600

www.ingramcontent.com/pod-product-compliance
Lightning Source LLC
Chambersburg PA
CBHW051217170526
45166CB00005B/1938